MW01092960

Basketry
of the Luzon Cordillera, Philippines

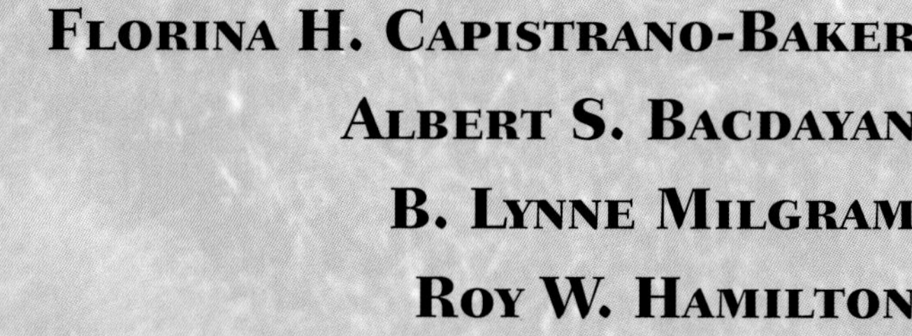

Florina H. Capistrano-Baker

Albert S. Bacdayan

B. Lynne Milgram

Roy W. Hamilton

BASKETRY

of the Luzon Cordillera, Philippines

UCLA FOWLER MUSEUM OF CULTURAL HISTORY · LOS ANGELES

This publication has been wholly supported by the volunteer staff of the Fowler Museum Store. Their considerable efforts are greatly appreciated.

Polly Svenson, Museum Store Manager
Sue Kallick, Assistant Store Manager
Simone Civet
Josey Dodd
Doris Finck
Elaine Fleischman
Helen Fowler
Moonlight Gurfield
Betsy Keliher
Marilyn Liebman
Roz Lipkis
Mickey Loy
Frances Martin
Nancy McCreery
Rosemary Murray
Ruth Parsell
Dona Rodensky
Helen Sjoberg
Nancy Stein
Hope Turney

Lynne Kostman and Michelle Ghaffari, Manuscript Editors
Lynne Kostman, Managing Editor
Sandy Bell, Designer
Don Cole, Principal Photographer
Daniel R. Brauer, Production Coordinator

UCLA Fowler Museum of Cultural History
Box 951549
Los Angeles, California 90095-1549

Printed and bound in Hong Kong
by South Sea International Press, Ltd.

FRONT COVER: cat. no. 26 (detail)
BACK COVER: fig. 3.13, cat. no. 31
PAGE 2: cat. no. 42 (detail)
PAGE 3: fig. 4.12
PAGE 4: fig. 4.9
PAGE 5: cat. nos. 9, 11
PAGE 7: cat. no. 7 (detail)

LIBRARY OF CONGRESS CATALOGING-IN-PUBLICATION DATA
Basketry of the Luzon Cordillera, Philippines / Florina H. Capistrano-Baker ... [et al.]
p. cm.
Catalog for an exhibition.
Includes bibliographical references.
ISBN 0-930741-66-8 (hard). — ISBN 0-930741-67-6 (soft)
1. Baskets, Igorot—Philippines—Luzon—Exhibitions. 2. Igorot (Philippine people)—Social life and customs—Exhibitions. 3. Basket making—Philippines—Luzon—Exhibitions. 4. Basket industry—Philippines—Luzon—Exhibitions. 5. University of California, Los Angeles. Fowler Museum of Cultural History--Exhibitions. I. Capistrano-Baker, Florina H. II. University of California, Los Angeles. Fowler Museum of Cultural History.
DS666.I2B37 1998
746.41′2′09599107479494—dc21 98-4286
CIP

Contents

Foreword

The collections of the UCLA Fowler Museum of Cultural History include nearly eight hundred items made by the various peoples inhabiting Luzon's Cordillera Central, or "central mountain range." Of these, roughly one quarter are baskets or related items—trays, hats, fish traps, and so forth—made with basketry materials and techniques. While other types of objects, notably the *bulul* rice god figures of the Ifugao and the patterned blankets of the Tinguian, or Itneg, people have received much more attention from art historians, the humble, but ubiquitous, items of basketry perhaps best capture in material form the unique ways of life of the agricultural peoples of the Cordillera.

Mirroring the varied roles that baskets play in Cordillera society, each of the three authors contributing to this book has approached the subject of Philippine basketry from a different perspective. First, Florina Capistrano-Baker, an art historian, provides an overview of the wide-ranging uses to which basketry items have been put by the various groups inhabiting the region. Next, anthropologist Albert Bacdayan focuses on a single cultural community, consisting of the western Bontoc villages of Fidelisan and Tanulong, and documents the complete repertoire of utilitarian basket types, as well as the sacred ancestral baskets known as *takba*. Finally, Lynne Milgram, also an anthropologist, considers Ifugao basketry from the point of view of its production in a changing economy.

The Luzon Cordillera today, like most parts of the developing world, is indeed undergoing rapid change. The precipitous terrain that once kept potential visitors at bay, and hence perpetuated distinctive ways of life, now instead draws outsiders to admire the beauty of the setting—in both its natural and cultural aspects. Some types of basketry, such as winnowing trays and fish traps, remain in constant demand and are still widely produced for local use. Others, notably the locust containers and cotton-harvesting baskets included in this catalog, have all but vanished as formerly important aspects of the traditional ways of procuring a livelihood have changed. This process of change is responsible for the diverse character of the photographic documentation in this book; some types of baskets can still be photographed in daily use, while others no longer have a place in day-to-day activities and can be presented only through historical photographs. Furthermore, because relatively little research has been directed toward the study of baskets, modern photos of basketry items in use are relatively scarce, while baskets show up coincidentally in a great many historical photographs intended to illustrate other subjects.

Almost all of the baskets in this catalog came to the Fowler Museum through the generosity of Helen and Dr. Robert Kuhn, who acquired them in the Philippines in the late 1970s. With the assistance of William Beyer, a son of the pioneering anthropologist H. Otley Beyer and, at the time, one of the leading dealers of Philippine art and craft materials, the Kuhns were able to collect examples of nearly every type of basketry made in the Cordillera. The timing was critical, as many of the older types were soon to become unavailable. The baskets were in fact being rapidly sold by owners who had either found industrially produced substitutes or who no longer engaged in activities for which the baskets had been required. These owners had made the decision to exchange their baskets for the one thing that was even more versatile in changing times: cash.

Unlike some of the baskets of Japan or of the native peoples of California and the Pacific Northwest, the basketry items in this catalog were not intended as art. The Kuhns were attracted to their simple beauty as functional objects, and this will undoubtedly be their primary appeal to others as well. Beyond the aesthetic pleasure they give, today they serve as an invaluable record of the unique ways of life—now undergoing rapid change—that were developed by the peoples of the Cordillera.

ROY W. HAMILTON
Curator of Southeast Asian and Oceanic Collections

Acknowledgments

This volume and the exhibition it accompanies stand as a tribute to the generosity and connoisseurship of Helen and Dr. Robert Kuhn. The Kuhns have been consistent supporters and great friends of the Fowler Museum of Cultural History since its inception. Many diverse portions of our collections, ranging from Philippine baskets to African musical instruments, have been immeasurably strengthened through the Kuhns' involvement. That this book is able to offer the first comprehensive treatment of its subject is entirely the result of the foresight and energy of this dedicated couple

The Museum also owes a debt of gratitude to volunteer Jovita Luglug, who assisted with this project in numerous ways. Through Jovita's efforts, we were able to gain the assistance of a number of people from the Cordillera in selecting and researching baskets for the exhibition, including Jerome Fagsao, Virgilio Inhumang, Munggolnon Bugatti, Miguel Sugguiyao, and Bugan Hettel. Jovita also made the arrangements for a curatorial visit to her hometown of Banaue, where additional assistance was provided by Lily Beyer Luglug and Hospicio Dulnuan. Michael Bermudez assisted with a preliminary inventory of the Fowler Museum's Cordillera basketry collection. Professor Harold Conklin of Yale University made many useful suggestions and shared some of his vast store of knowledge and experience in the Ifugao region. Charles LeNoir made his photographs available to augment those provided by Professor Conklin and each of the contributing authors.

In addition to Helen and Dr. Robert Kuhn, we would like to acknowledge the efforts of Jill and Barry Kitnick, Mr. and Mrs. Louis Marienthal, the late Alan Rose, the Rogers Family Foundation, the Ventura County Museum of Art and History, and Manus (the support group of the Fowler Museum) for donating or loaning the baskets that are featured in this catalog.

DORAN H. ROSS
Director

ROY W. HAMILTON
Curator of Southeast Asian and Oceanic Collections

Notes on Orthography

There is no single established orthographic standard for writing the languages of the Cordillera. Furthermore, the pronunciation of terms often varies from village to village within a single language area. In some cases, spellings that do not match contemporary orthographic standards have become thoroughly established in the literature (for example, *Bontoc* rather than *Bontok*).

The catalog records of the UCLA Fowler Museum of Cultural History were used as the basic source for the names of baskets that appear in this book. Most of these terms originally came from William Beyer. In a few instances these names have been changed or the spelling adjusted when recommended by native speakers of the languages involved, including elders who were interviewed about the baskets. Bontoc and Ifugao terms were further checked against the most authoritative dictionaries (Reid 1976; Newell 1993). Professor Harold C. Conklin kindly provided additional comments on orthography.

ROY W. HAMILTON

FIGURE I.I
Houses in the Bontoc village of Bayyu cluster on a slope beside the community's terraced rice lands. 1997.

CHAPTER 1

Containing Life: Philippine Basketry Traditions on the Cordillera

Florina H. Capistrano-Baker

BASKETRY IN CORDILLERA SOCIETY

The inhabitants of the Cordillera Central, or "central mountain range," on the northern Philippine island of Luzon are generally known as Igorots, a generic term applied to members of a number of ethnolinguistic groups. The origin of the word "Igorot" is not entirely clear. While some believe the appellation to be of Spanish origin, William Henry Scott (1966, 155–56), an American missionary scholar who lived among the Igorots, argues that it is probably an indigenous word that originally had none of the negative connotations it later came to acquire.[1]

The groups most commonly identified as Igorot include the Ifugao, Bontoc, Kalinga, Tinguian, Ibaloi, Kankanay, Isneg, Gaddang, and Ilongot. There is some disagreement, however, about the groups that should be included under this rubric and the correct names for them. Like many non-Western cultures, the inhabitants of the Cordillera originally identified themselves by using the word for *people* or by referring to their home village; hence, discrepancies exist among the names imposed on them by outsiders. Even today, old men belonging to the group identified as Ifugao do not distinguish themselves by that name. In fact, they are referred to by other highlanders as Ikiangan, or "people of Kiangan," an Ifugao village (Ellis 1981, 184; Scott 1966, 166).

The Igorots reside in the northern part of the island of Luzon (fig. 1.4), largely concentrated in the former Mountain Province (which has been subdivided into the present-day provinces of Ifugao, Benguet, Kalinga, Apayao, and Mountain Province [formerly Bontoc]) and in Abra Province. The groups represented in this exhibition are the Ifugao, Bontoc, Tinguian, Ibaloi, Kalinga, and Kankanay.

Agricultural lands are among the most valuable possessions of the peoples of the Cordillera (figs. 1.1, 1.2). Among the Ifugao, rice fields were traditionally their only form of real estate, for houses could be dismantled and transferred elsewhere when they were bought or sold (Barton 1922, 402). In fact, Ifugao social structure is traditionally based on the ownership of rice fields. Although variations exist within different groups, there are generally three classes.

FIGURE 1.2
A water buffalo is used to churn the mud in preparation for planting a rice terrace. The man at the center submerges freshly cut wild sunflower plants in the mud; these will decay and fertilize the growing rice crop. At the upper left, another worker transplants rice seedlings in a newly prepared field. Bayyu, Mountain Province, 1997.

FIGURE 1.3
Baskets are used in every stage of the harvesting, processing, and storing of rice. Here a man works at a communal mortar site in a Kalinga village, pounding rice to remove the hull. His supply of rice, still on the dried stalks, fills a round basket in front of him. The mortar is a deep hole in the rock, perhaps in use for generations. Lubu, Kalinga, 1978.

FIGURE 1.4 (OPPOSITE)
Map of the Luzon Cordillera.

Wealth, among the Ifugao, is traditionally a function of the yield of the rice fields that one owns. An abundant harvest and extensive holdings enable the attainment of the highest level of status. To reach this level, one must also sponsor a festival known as *uya-uy* and host an expensive feast after having supervised the carving of a monumental wooden bench called *hagabi*. The middle class consists of people who usually have enough rice to eat but run out toward the end of the agricultural year and must borrow from the upper class. At harvest time, they are constrained to repay the borrowed rice twofold within two to three months. Those with very small rice fields or none at all are considered very poor and are relegated to the lowest class.[2]

Basketry plays an indispensable role in practically all aspects of Igorot life. It is, in fact, one of the most ubiquitous crafts of the Cordillera. There are baskets to cradle the newborn infant, vessels for daily and ritual use, and containers for human remains. Plaited winnowing trays, carrying baskets, and covered containers facilitate the harvesting, transporting, storing, and serving of grains, tubers, and legumes for nourishment and survival (figs. 1.3, 1.5; cat. nos. 1, 4–9, 11, 13, 17–21). Basketry hats and rain capes protect against sun and rain (fig. 1.6; cat. nos. 41–43). Twined and plaited traps and sieves help in catching

Pacific Ocean
North
W
E
S
ILOCOS NORTE
APAYAO
CAGAYAN
ABRA
KALINGA
ILOCOS SUR
MOUNTAIN PROVINCE
ISABELA
IFUGAO
LA UNION
BENGUET
NUEVA VIZCAYA
AURORA
Cordillera Central
Isneg
Tinguian
Kalinga
Bontoc
Gaddang
Ifugao
Kankanay
Ibaloi
Ilongot
Laoag
Kabugao
Abulug River (Apayao)
Chico River
Cagayan River
Abra River
Magat River
Bangued
Vigan
Tuguegarao
Tabuk
Lubuagan
Ilagan
Fidelisan
Tanulong
Sagada
Bontoc
Samoki
Kanyu
Ambawan
Bayyu
Madukayan
Barlig
Cambulo
Mayaoyao
Mt. Polis
Banaue
Lagawe
Kiangan
San Fernando
Mt. Pulog
Bayombong
Baguio
0
25 miles
Manila
PHILIPPINES

fish, shellfish, and insect foods (fig. 1.7; cat. nos. 33–40). Assorted basketry bags and pouches carry personal items, such as betel-chewing[3] supplies or tobacco-related paraphernalia (cat. nos. 49, 50); packed lunches and snacks (cat. nos. 10, 12, 14); and potent amulets (cat. no. 48). As Philippine basketry specialist Robert Lane (1986, 15) notes, baskets can be fully understood only by studying the purpose for which they were made, for their function informs the logic of their structure.

Cordillera baskets range in form and size from small carrying pouches to large trays and jarlike vessels. They are almost always made of bamboo, rattan, or a combination of the two. The most commonly used material is a vinelike bamboo called *anes* or *anis*, which is distinguished from the upright, treelike bamboo. The most frequently utilized construction technique is plaiting, although twining and coiling are also used. The average Igorot household normally requires at least one large winnowing tray and a variety of smaller, jar-shaped or box-shaped vessels to store food (Scott 1966, 105).

FIGURE 1.5
Baskets are also used for serving rice. This Ifugao family gathers at mealtime around a square, lidded basket (*hū'up*) filled with cooked rice. Carved wooden bowls hold the side dishes, including peas and snails. The family's supply of utensils is kept in a spoon basket (*ayyud*) visible at the upper right.

FIGURE 1.6 (OPPOSITE)
An Ifugao work group repairs rice terrace walls. One man wears a plaited hat (*lido*), which can serve to protect from sun or rain.

Basketmaking is gender specific among some Igorot groups but not among others. Among the Ifugao, for example, both men and women engage in basketmaking. But among the Kalinga of Madukayan barrio, all weaving of rattan or bamboo is done only by men. Kalinga boys learn to make baskets through play and imitation. One of first skills they acquire is the weaving of basketry fish traps, which they use in play and in serious food gathering. As they make the transition to adulthood, these boys must master the manufacture of all other items necessary for normal daily living, from the making of grass raincoats to the construction of houses (Barton 1922, 423; Scott 1966, 104–5).

FIGURE 1.7
An Ifugao man sets a basketry fish trap by burying it in the mud of a flooded rice terrace. Small fish, which normally hide in cavities in the mud, enter the trap through a conical opening at the wide end. The opening at the narrow end, through which the fish will be removed when the trap is lifted, is plugged with leaves. Tam-an village, Banaue, 1997.

Basketry objects are also manufactured for trade with the lowlands. Typical trade items include backpacks, hunting bags, and trays. Basketry is traded locally within the Cordillera as well. One widely distributed type, for example—first described by Fray Francisco Antolin in 1789—is a kind of tightly woven basket with two overlapping compartments. This basket was always carried about to serve as a container for the little scales used to measure gold dust for barter, and it could also be used as a pillow at night when traveling (Scott 1974, 4–5, 13, 181–84, 334). Probably similar to catalog number 50, this and other forms of Cordillera basketry such as pouches (cat. no. 49) and backpacks (cat. nos. 23–26) became fashionable among non-Igorot lowlanders in the 1970s as postcolonial statements of national identity.

In their traditional context, Cordillera baskets serve multiple functions. Winnowing trays and sieves double as serving trays for cooked rice and tubers. Hunters' backpacks and women's baskets carry provisions to work and later transport freshly gathered foods back to the village. Women's rain capes double as carrying baskets, while men's hats provide storage for personal paraphernalia.

Social roles and group affiliations are also revealed in the different basketry shapes and styles, which are often gender and group specific. Most importantly, baskets contain the ritual nourishment and daily sustenance that are essential to good health and survival. These plaited, twined, and coiled vessels fulfill numerous practical, ritual, and aesthetic needs.

THE HISTORICAL CONTEXT

Cordillera baskets, sculpture, weapons, and textiles are among the most well represented of all the Philippine art forms in American museums today. Interest in the Cordillera among Western scholars specializing in the Philippines is enhanced by the large body of colonial research that exists for this region when compared to most other areas in the Philippines and by the presence of substantial collections of late nineteenth- to early twentieth-century Cordillera material in European and American museums.

The specific historical events leading to this phenomenon, however, are only vaguely remembered in America today. Many Americans are unaware that the Philippines were once a colony of the United States. Visitors to this exhibition might, therefore, well wonder what the 1998 Philippine Centennial is all about and why it is being celebrated in exhibitions throughout the United States.

Briefly, the Philippines became known to the Western world in 1521 when the Portuguese explorer Ferdinand Magellan set sail in the name of King Charles of Spain to find a westward route to the fabled Spice Islands. In the course of his voyage, he stumbled upon an archipelago, previously unknown in the West, which he claimed for the Spanish Crown. Initially called Archipelago de San Lazaro, the newly "discovered" islands were later renamed Las Islas Filipinas, after King Philip II of Spain.

In 1896, after over three centuries of Spanish rule, the inhabitants of the Philippines rose up in Revolution and proclaimed their independence on

12 June 1898. Although Filipino insurgents had already liberated most of the country, Spain nonetheless ceded it to the United States in exchange for twenty million dollars on 10 December 1898 in the course of negotiations that ended the Spanish-American War. Thus, the 1998 Centennial celebration of Philippine Independence ironically coincides with the 100th anniversary of the Spanish-American War and American colonization of the islands. The Philippines remained an American colony until they were finally granted independence on 4 July 1946.

America's experiment with colonialism generated an impassioned debate at home between aspiring imperialists and ardent anti-imperialists. At one end of the political spectrum, President William McKinley justified the invasion of the Philippines with the notion of "manifest destiny," revealing to a group of clergymen that God had told him to annex the islands and "do the best we could for them." Echoing this sentiment, Rudyard Kipling wrote a poem titled "The White Man's Burden" and subtitled "The United States and the Philippine Islands," which exhorted Americans to "take up the White Man's burden" and bestow the blessings of their civilization on the "new-caught, sullen peoples, half devil and half child" (Karnow 1989, 11, 136ff.; Kipling 1899).

Eminent figures such as Mark Twain, then at the peak of his fame, strenuously objected to America's imperialistic venture. Abolitionists equated the subjugation of people overseas with slavery, while legal specialists cautioned that colonialism violated the fundamental American constitutional principle of "government by consent of the governed" (Karnow 1989, 11).

The ubiquitous references to "heathens" and "savages" are particularly ironic, for about 80 percent of the population of the Philippines at the time were devout Catholics (the first conversions dated back to the sixteenth century following initial contact with Spain). Several key leaders of the Philippine nationalist movement were, in fact, members of a multilingual elite educated at local and European universities. In order to justify the United States colonization of the islands, however, it was necessary to construct an image of a "primitive" subaltern, a people incapable of governing themselves. Thus, it was the unconquered, unconverted, unacculturated minority groups of the northern and southern regions who figured prominently in colonial accounts, photographs, and expositions.

Within this politically charged context, the Igorots of the Cordillera Central were singled out for particular scrutiny. They were the subject of frequent books, monographs, and articles. These often bore sensational titles, as exemplified by the essay "Head-Hunters of Northern Luzon," published in *National Geographic Magazine*, in which the United States Philippine Commissioner Dean C. Worcester declared that "all but one of these tribes ... [had], until recently, engaged in headhunting" (1912, 833). Even scholarly publications featured melodramatic titles such as *Taming the Philippine Headhunters* (Keesing and Keesing 1934).

Cordillera peoples were brought to America and exhibited at the Louisiana Purchase Exposition held in Saint Louis in 1904 to celebrate the newly consolidated empire. The negative impact of such displays was not lost upon mainstream Christian Filipinos. During the Spanish colonial period, Filipino nationalist Dr. José Rizal had protested against a similar exhibition of Igorots at the *Exposicion de Las Islas Filipinas* in Madrid in 1887: "It is no Exposition of the Philippines at all but only of Igorots, who will play music, do their cooking, and sing and dance.... I worked hard against this degradation of my fellow Filipinos that they should not be exhibited among the animals and plants!" (Scott 1974, 276).

Filipinos objected to such displays planned subsequent to the Louisiana Purchase Exposition. Nonetheless, the exhibition of "savages" from the Philippines continued, firmly establishing the image of a backward people dependent upon America's benevolence—a notion not easily dispelled.[4] Anthropologists dispatched to the islands at the beginning of the twentieth century to gather information and assemble collections for American institutions also focused on the highland groups.

This somewhat skewed perspective persists as contemporary scholars build upon collections and scholarship pioneered by American colonial officials and early ethnographers. Consequently, the peoples of the Cordillera are among the most well documented of Philippine groups—both in the colonial literature and in American collections today.

CONTAINING LIFE: SUSTENANCE AND SURVIVAL

Although baskets are manufactured throughout the Philippines and are indispensable in a host of daily activities, for the reasons noted above, early collectors were particularly attracted to Cordillera baskets. As a consequence, they were acquired in larger quantities than those from other regions. Although not all basketry types survive today, baskets continue to be of universal importance on the Cordillera. Members of all social classes utilize an assortment of baskets, the quality of which varies with the wealth of the owner.

As noted earlier, baskets are particularly useful in agricultural activities. Rice and sweet potatoes, or camotes, supplemented by legumes and meat, are the main sources of nourishment on the Cordillera. An especially wide array of basket forms are associated with the cultivation of rice, ranging from carrying baskets used in harvesting to winnowing trays, serving plates, and assorted covered vessels employed to store hulled, boiled, or roasted rice (cat. nos. 1–14).

Among the Ifugao, heavy work in the rice fields involving the manipulation of soil, water, and rocks is done by men. This includes the construction, repair, and maintenance of rice terrace walls. Women, on the other hand, are primarily responsible for planting and transplanting rice, weeding, and harvesting. Specific practices, however, vary in different regions.

Harvesting is usually done in groups, beginning with a prayer for bountiful harvest addressed to the rice deity. Bundles of harvested stalks are tied with short lengths of *anes*, which have been prepared beforehand. Among the Bontoc, the bundles are then stacked in carrying baskets called *gimáta*, which are secured to either end of a pole that is carried by the men across their shoul-

FIGURE 1.8
The double basket (*gimáta*) is the standard carrying basket of Bontoc men. One of its most important uses is in transporting newly harvested rice from the fields back to the village. Reproduced from Jenks (1905, pl. cxx).

FIGURE 1.9
Women normally carry heavy baskets on top of their heads. Here a Kalinga woman carries rice from a granary to her home. Lubu, Kalinga, 1978.

FIGURE 1.10
Ifugao women pull rice grains from the dried stalks in preparation for making rice beer. Threshing is typically done by hand in this manner. Banaue, 1997.

ders (fig. 1.8; cat. no. 1). In contrast, women usually carry a single basket on the head (fig. 1.9; cat. no. 20).

The newly harvested rice bundles are transported back to the village in the baskets and spread out in the sun to dry. Another invocation is performed to keep the harvest safe and sufficient before the rice is piled into the granary (Scott 1966, 20–21, 106–7, 229).

Before cooking, the rice must be threshed to separate the grain from the stalk (fig. 1.10). The grain is then pounded with a heavy wooden pestle in a large stone or wooden mortar to remove the hull. The hulled rice is transferred to winnowing trays to facilitate removal of the chaff. Bontoc winnowing trays (*lig-o*) are round (cat. no. 3), while Ifugao trays (*liga-u*) are traditionally square (cat. no. 2). Winnowing trays may also be used for a variety of other functions, such as processing crops (fig. 1.11) or serving communal meals of rice and meat or soup.

After winnowing, the rice is either cooked in boiling water or stored for later use. The Bontoc store hulled rice in elegant jarlike containers called *kamuwan* (cat. nos. 6, 7). The Ifugao version of this container is a graceful vessel called *ulbung*, one of the few types of Cordillera baskets constructed using the coiling technique (figs. 1.12, 1.13; cat. nos. 4, 5). The jarlike shape of both *kamuwan* and *ulbung* derives from the contours of imported Chinese ceramic vessels, which are treasured heirlooms.

Ceramic containers imported from China, Vietnam, Thailand, and Japan have long been valued by many indigenous groups in Island Southeast Asia for their rarity, beauty, and durability. In the past, trade ceramics were used by many island cultures as currency and for ritual purposes. Such vessels were often interred with deceased persons of high rank. Wooden lids or stoppers and protective basketry sheathing were often added to the containers as they were adapted for local use (cat. no. 15; Capistrano-Baker 1994, 47).

Imported jars were often given names and extraordinary powers were ascribed to them as they were handed down through several generations. When the American anthropologist Fay-Cooper Cole (Cole and Laufer 1912, 12) visited the Tinguian, for example, he continually heard tales of a wonderful jar called "Magsawi," which was said to have the ability to talk like a human being. Moreover, a Tinguian's wealth was largely reckoned by the number of imported ceramic vessels that he owned (fig. 1.14). Among the Kalinga, imported Chinese and Japanese jars called *gusi* were the most valued heirlooms. These were kept on a special shelf known as *pagud*; a guest was supposed to note the position of the *pagud* so as not to sit with his back toward it (Barton 1949, 102).

The use of Chinese jars on the Cordillera is documented in early reports such as those by the German pharmacist Alexander Schadenberg (1889, 677), who relates seeing imported ceramic vessels used for storing rice beer and jar-

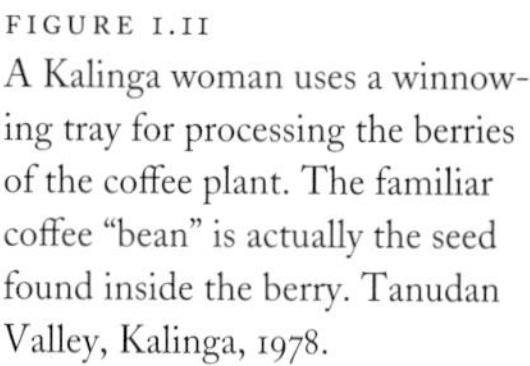

FIGURE 1.11
A Kalinga woman uses a winnowing tray for processing the berries of the coffee plant. The familiar coffee "bean" is actually the seed found inside the berry. Tanudan Valley, Kalinga, 1978.

FIGURE 1.12
An Ifugao man fills a jar-shaped rice storage basket (*ulbung*) from a supply of freshly hulled and winnowed rice in a winnowing tray. Hulling rice and refilling the *ulbung* is an activity that is normally repeated every day.

FIGURE 1.13
The *ulbung* has a handle that allows it to hang from hooks (*kinahu*). These hooks are carved in the shape of a dog and attached to the underside of a special shelf (*halada'*) located near the hearth inside an Ifugao home. Hanging the *ulbung* in this fashion keeps rice dry and free from pests. Day Collection, Fowler Museum of Cultural History.

FIGURE 1.14
Collection of imported ceramic jars belonging to a wealthy Tinguian in Abra. In the center is the famous "talking jar" called "Magsawi." Reproduced from Cole and Laufer (1912, pl. 3).

shaped basketry versions used to store a variety of other objects (Scott 1974, 313). Small ceramic jars such as the Ifugao *hinoghogan* are traditionally used to contain smaller amounts of rice beer for use in a ceremonial context (cat. no. 15).

An integral part of religious rituals and agricultural festivities, rice beer (also known as rice wine) consists primarily of glutinous rice and homemade yeast.[5] An average batch of fermented rice beer sufficient to fill a medium-size ceramic jar requires fifteen bundles of rice. After the grain is threshed, hulled, and winnowed, it is toasted in an iron vat over an outdoor fire. The rice is then transferred to basketry trays, the vat filled with water, and the rice poured back in to boil. A yeast ball made from crushed plant roots is mixed into the warm, cooked rice, which has been spread out in winnowing trays. The mixture is transferred into a basket or trough lined with banana leaves and sealed for initial fermentation. After three days, the mash and fermented liquids are transferred to a ceramic jar and covered tightly with banana leaves. The beer can be moved to smaller containers after another five or six days of fermentation (Conklin 1980, 22–23). One means of accomplishing this transfer is to plunge a tubular bamboo sieve into the jar, thus causing the fermented liquid to flow into the center of the sieve while keeping the mash on the outside (cat. no. 16). The strained liquid is then withdrawn with a bamboo dipper.

Sugar cane juice or water may be added to increase the quantity of beer, although this alters its taste and strength. Because the fermenting plants used differ from place to place, rice drinks made by the Kalinga, Bontoc, and Ifugao vary greatly in quality and flavor (Scott 1966, 75–76).

Among the Bontoc, food is served on ceremonial occasions in individual basketry plates called *giyag* (cat. no. 13), while the large winnowing trays called *liga-u* (cat. no. 2) are sometimes used for communal meals among the Ifugao. The Bontoc use distinctive containers called *lóden*, which consist of a coconut-shell vessel fitted with a wooden lid and reinforced with rattan openwork basketry, to store smaller portions of meat (cat. no. 27). Luxurious covered baskets, such as the square Ifugao *hū'up* (cat. no. 8), and larger or more elaborate

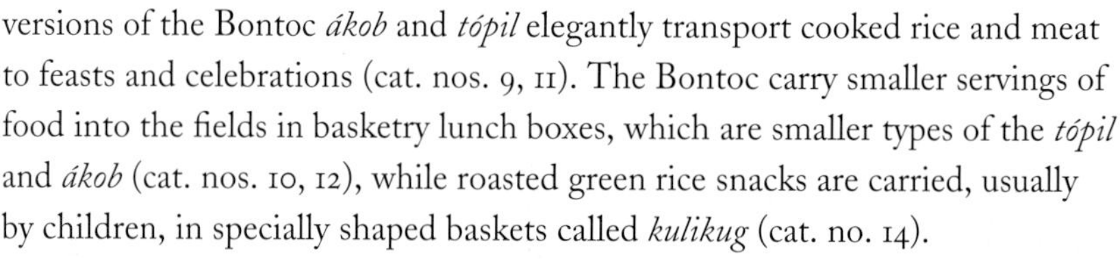

versions of the Bontoc *ákob* and *tópil* elegantly transport cooked rice and meat to feasts and celebrations (cat. nos. 9, 11). The Bontoc carry smaller servings of food into the fields in basketry lunch boxes, which are smaller types of the *tópil* and *ákob* (cat. nos. 10, 12), while roasted green rice snacks are carried, usually by children, in specially shaped baskets called *kulikug* (cat. no. 14).

While rice is the most prestigious staple and ritual food on the Cordillera, sweet potatoes, or camotes, provide food for the majority of the Igorot population. More easily cultivated than rice, camotes can be grown almost anywhere. They provide sustenance not only for people but also for domestic animals. Leaves of camote vines and camote parings are boiled and fed to hogs, and sometimes camotes themselves are used as animal feed. In Ifugao about twenty to thirty varieties of camotes are cultivated. Because they are so commonly available, they are not considered a high-status food. In fact, to say that someone has only camotes to eat is an indication of poverty (Barton 1922, 399–400).

As with newly harvested rice, camotes are carried from the fields back to the villages in basketry containers constructed specifically for this purpose. And as with the various rice containers and winnowing trays, the style and shape of camote baskets vary among different Igorot groups. A trumpet-shaped container called *kayabang* with a round flaring rim that tapers to a truncated base, for example, is used by Ibaloi women for transporting camotes, yams, taro, and cassava (cat. no. 17). The Ifugao version, called *balyag* (cat. no. 18), is similarly flared at the top but has a square profile in contrast to the rounded contours of the Ibaloi basket. Both types of vessels are carried by means of a strap worn across the forehead and are used exclusively by women (fig. 1.15). A variation on the Ifugao *balyag* is a shorter, four-cornered basket called *allataw*, which is also used to carry various tubers (cat. no. 19).

FIGURE 1.15
An Ibaloi woman carries rice stalks in a basket on her back, secured with a strap across the forehead. Reproduced from Moss (1920, pl. 37).

FIGURE 1.16
Plaited chicken coops (*ubi*) hang from the floor beam of an Ifugao house. Reproduced from Barton (1930, pl. xxv).

Among the Kalinga, sturdy round baskets called *awit* (cat. no. 20) are used to transport newly harvested tubers, rice, or vegetables. Unlike baskets with forehead straps, these round baskets are worn directly on top of the head. Tinguian women also carry harvest baskets directly on their heads, such as the basket for vegetables called *labba* (cat. no. 21).

Basketry containers are indispensable not only in agriculture but also in hunting and gathering. Hunters embark on their expeditions with a plaited backpack filled with provisions to be consumed on the way and replaced with meat after a successful hunt. One version of the Ifugao backpack, called *inabnūtan*, is covered with a thick overlay of palm fibers to repel rain (cat. no. 23). Versions without this decorative waterproofing might incorporate heavy rattan hoops, not unlike the aluminum frames on contemporary Western backpacks, that allow the baskets to double as portable stools. This is the case with the Ifugao *hapē'eng* (cat. no. 25). Like the *hapē'eng*, the Bontoc backpack called *sangi* features a plaited receptacle with heavy rattan shoulder straps (cat. no. 26).

Cordillera baskets are also a means to protect and transport domestic animals. Chickens, pigs, goats, and cattle are the most commonly raised animals in the region. Chickens and pigs are considered the most important of these animals and are carefully tended. Among the Ifugao, for example, the owner knows every single chicken in his flock. While chickens roam freely during the day, they are collected every night in special basketry coops called *ubi*, which are hung under the eaves of the house to protect them from rats, cats, and thieves (fig. 1.16; cat. no. 31; Barton 1922, 421).

The attention and care given to chickens reflect their significance not only as a major source of food but also as important sacrificial animals. Among the Ifugao, chickens are sacrificed in various rituals associated with warfare or healing. They are traditionally transported to the ceremonial site in special openwork baskets called *alubī'ub* (cat. no. 32). Chickens are also traditionally exchanged for rice. In the early twentieth century, a chicken was worth anywhere from five to twenty rice bundles during the growing season and from ten to forty bundles at harvest time (Barton 1922, 429).

Smaller animal foods such as fish and snails are traditionally caught with the help of basketry sieves, traps, and containers (cat. nos. 33, 38–40). Ifugao women use plaited sieves to scoop up edible snails, which are considered delicacies, from the rice paddies after the harvest (cat. no. 33). Bontoc women invariably wear a small, rounded basket called *aggawin* around their hips when working in the paddies (cat. no. 34). This basket usually contains lunch and is later filled with mollusks and crustaceans picked up in the wet fields or gathered in the river to be brought back home (Jenks 1905, 87, 121–22).

Smaller fish are similarly gathered in the rice paddies after the rice harvest, a task frequently entrusted to children. As with Kalinga boys, who first learn the art of basketmaking by weaving fish traps for play and food gathering, Ifugao children learn to gather food through imitation and play. Bontoc boys as young as six to ten years old can capture a hundred or more of the small fish known as *kacho* by hand (Jenks 1905, 85–86). Ifugao children are often responsible for setting small, globular fish traps called *gūbu* at dusk and collecting them in the morning (cat. no. 38). Larger fish are caught in streams and rivers using a waisted cylindrical trap with a flared mouth, also called *gūbu*, into which the fish are carried by the current (cat. no. 39). A trap specifically designed for catching eels is the *udal*, an attenuated bamboo tube that features a spring mechanism that snaps shut as the eels pass through the mouth of the trap (cat. no. 40).

Like edible snails, locusts were traditionally considered a delicacy on the Cordillera. In the past, swarms of locusts frequently visited the highlands and were greeted by shouts to alert all the villagers. Armed with nets, men, women, and children would rush out to capture the insects. The locusts were kept alive in jarlike baskets with open-slatted sides or a netlike bottom for ventilation. Locusts were prepared for food by boiling. After the wings and feet were removed, they were dried in the sun until brittle, pounded into a powder, and then stored away in tightly covered bamboo tubes (Barton 1922, 395).

The Ifugao locust basket, called *butit*, is constructed of bamboo slats twined with rattan lashing, creating open-slatted sides that allow air to circulate (cat. no. 37). In contrast, the Kalinga version, called *bocus*, has tightly woven sides with ventilation provided at the bottom of the basket (cat. no. 36). Another type of locust container utilizing twined bamboo slats is the Bontoc *iwus* (cat. no. 35), which has a jarlike configuration similar to the Kalinga *bocus*. This type of basket is rarely found today. Besides locusts, three species of dragonflies, as well as crickets and beetles, were traditionally used as food by the Ifugao (Barton 1922, 395).

BASKETRY AS PROTECTION: TEMPORAL AND DIVINE

Just as basketry containers safeguard food supplies and domestic animals, basketry clothing and accessories provide protection for people. Plaited hats and waterproof basketry capes shelter their wearers against inclement weather. Bontoc and Ifugao men shield themselves from frequent rains by means of plaited basketry capes with multiple layers of palm fiber or grass (cat. no. 41). Similarly, Kalinga men make and wear rain capes made of palm leaves attached to a ropelike strand tied around the neck; the leaves thus form a giant protective ruff (Scott 1966, 83).

In contrast, women generally do not wear the fiber or grass cape. Instead they use a scoop-shaped basket constructed of palm leaves and reinforced with a double framework of rattan, which they wear inverted over the head (cat. no. 42). When not serving as protection from rain, the same basket can be utilized for carrying camotes and other items.

Various types of basketry hats indicate social status and group affiliation (fig. 1.17). A married Bontoc man, for example, wears a small, coiled hat that is undecorated except for a central protuberance embellished with a tuft of horse or human hair (cat. no. 44). The Bontoc bachelor's hat, in contrast, is flat at the top and more colorful, made with red-dyed rattan or fabric and decorated with boars' tusks, dogs' teeth, and chicken feathers (cat. no. 46).

Kalinga hats tend to be even more elaborately decorated with geometric designs and in some areas, with beads (cat. no. 47). Among the Kalinga of Madukayan, an ornate version of the hat—decorated with brilliant red, yellow, and black paint derived from bark and berries—is considered a suitable "courtship gift" from a young man to a girl. Until the early twentieth century, Kalinga men had a secondary use for these hats: they carried personal items, such as tobacco or betel supplies, safely tucked inside them on top of the head.

FIGURE 1.17
These Bontoc men wear hats (*soklong*) made with the coiled basketry technique. The plain hats identify them as married men. Shortly after this photograph was taken, the men removed their hats, revealing where they kept their smoking supplies and other personal items. Bontoc town, Mountain Province, 1997.

Today, however, a red cloth bag suspended from the neck is more commonly used to carry such paraphernalia (Scott 1966, 84).

Smoking and betel chewing are among the most important luxuries for several groups on the Cordillera. Ifugao women carry their betel-chewing supplies and other personal paraphernalia in a flat pouch, called *upig*, which is tucked into a fold at the top of the wraparound skirt (cat. no. 49). Ifugao men, however, carry their betel and tobacco in a woven cloth bag.

Among the Ifugao, chewing betel is an important social ritual, practiced even by the poorest. A common salutation is "give me an areca nut," which is answered with "all right, where is your lime box" or "your betel leaf." Thus, social interaction is facilitated by sharing one's supplies. Betel chewing is also an important component of religious rituals. Ingredients for the betel chew are offered to deities in ritual feasts, and betel is chewed during marriage ceremonies (Barton 1922, 407).

The Bontoc, by contrast, do not ordinarily chew betel. Bontoc men traditionally carry their smoking supplies in a saddle-shaped basket, called *kupit*, which has separate compartments for tobacco, a packed lunch, and small valuables (cat. no. 50).

Basketry provides physical protection not only in the form of clothing and accessories but also as the ultimate shelter, the house. Early Spanish descriptions of Igorot houses depict them as generally low and windowless, designed to provide warmth in the cool highlands. These structures were elevated about three feet above the ground with their four-sided roofs almost touching the ground. Fires kept burning in open hearths all night provided warmth and illumination. There were traditionally no furnishings except for locally manufactured baskets, pots, wooden plates, and the prestigious Chinese jars (Scott 1974, 175–76).

Although house types vary among different Igorot groups, house construction often incorporates basketry techniques. The typical Kalinga house in Madukayan, for example, has a wooden framework of supporting posts, floor joists, and roof beams, and its basketry walls are made of split-and-plaited bamboo. It is raised off the ground with its floor about chest height. The floor joists support smaller transverse beams placed parallel to one another about three inches apart, on top of which a floor of split bamboo is laid, which can easily be removed for washing. Two doorways at opposite sides of the house are closed at night or during storms by basketry panels made to slide horizontally on a bamboo track or, less frequently, hinged to swing inward and upward (Scott 1966, 77–78). Traditional Bontoc and Ifugao houses similarly feature basketry walls and fiber roofs (fig. 1.18).

Basketry also provides divine protection. Cordillera notions of the supernatural vary from group to group.[6] The Ifugao traditionally have the largest recorded pantheon of deities with no one considered supreme. The Bontoc and Kankanay traditionally practice a form of monotheism, while the Tinguian and Kalinga believe in a supreme deity called Kabunian, also known as Kadaklan, or "The Greatest." The culture hero Lumawig is also associated with the deity Kabunian among different groups. Spirits of departed ancestors,

FIGURE 1.18
The plaited bamboo walls of these Ifugao houses are worked with twill patterns. Reproduced from Barton (1919, pl. 17).

called *anito*, are thought to concern themselves with the daily affairs of the living. They must therefore be placated and manipulated with sacrificial offerings (Barton 1949, 17–20).

Among the Ifugao, illness and death, as well as success in warfare, hunting, and agriculture, are believed to be the results of divine intervention. Hence, religious ceremonies are of crucial importance in obtaining good weather, good crops, and good health. Several agricultural rituals, expensive religious feasts, and healing ceremonies are performed each year. Because success in hunting is attributed to resident spirits of the hunting ground, sacrifices are necessary to induce the spirits to give up the game. Obtaining sacrificial animals such as pigs, chickens, ducks, and water buffalo for these numerous ritual feasts is a primary economic concern of the men of the village (Barton 1922, 389, 393).

Among many groups offerings are carried to the ritual site in basketry containers. Sacrificial fowl and pigs are transported to the ceremonial grounds in special carrying baskets (cat. no. 32), while rice beer to be used as part of the ritual offering may be transported in ceramic containers encased in protective rattan sheathing (cat. no. 15). Similarly, copper alloy gongs called *gangsa*, which provide instrumental music for ceremonial performances, are often brought to the dancing grounds in open-weave baskets created specifically for this purpose (cat. no. 30).

Instrumental music and dance performances are a prominent part of ceremonies associated with agriculture, hunting, and warfare. Among the Bontoc, the *gangsa* is the primary musical instrument. There are two types of *gangsa* in the Bontoc area, one larger and thicker than the other. The larger gong produces a bell-like and usually higher pitched tone. These gongs, the origin of which is not entirely clear, are highly prized and seldom sold to outsiders. There is no dancing without *gangsa* music. Bontoc men usually dance while playing the *gangsa*, while women perform rhythmic steps with extended arms, their blankets thrown about them, and their feet scarcely leaving the ground (Jenks 1905, 189–90, 193).

Another means of securing divine favor is through the use of various small objects believed to be imbued with supernatural powers. Such objects could include a special stone, a piece of glass or bone, a lump of meat, or some animal fat. Because of the extraordinary powers attributed to them, such objects serve as charms for various purposes. Among the Ifugao, a *kiwil*, for example, is believed to make one invulnerable to hostile weapons, while an *agayok* is a love charm used by men to attract women. These charms are frequently encased in rattan sheathing and carried in one's pocket, bag, or loincloth (cat. no. 48).

During illness or following an injury, the Bontoc healer makes use of a special carrying basket to bring a live chicken and a small amount of rice and wine to the spot where the ailing person was injured or taken ill. Pointing a stick in various directions, he attempts to call back the sick person's wandering soul, as illness and injuries are believed to be caused by a spirit, or *anito*, that has lured one's soul away (Jenks 1905, 199).

In Ifugao soul-trapping ceremonies associated with death in warfare, the ritual specialist ties a little palm leaf basket containing areca nuts, chicken blood, a piece of liver, and a little wine to a stick and goes toward the enemy region. If a bee, fly, or dragonfly—believed to be an enemy soul—is attracted by the bait, it is brought back in triumph and imprisoned in a bamboo tube. The men gather around large, flat baskets containing boiled rice and cooked meat from animal sacrifices. The ritual specialist blows the rising steam toward the enemy region, chanting:

> Ye are blown upon, Rice, Chicken, and Pig Flesh. Cool, but do not cool the lives of us who have lost a head. Cool the remembrance of our enemies, that our young men may meet them in the middle of the road. . . . Do not disseminate, but go upstream to the hills of our enemies. Enter their nostrils that they may rejoice in ye, thinking ye the savor of their own witchcraft ceremonials! They will continually die off; whilst we shall flourish as the banyan tree. [Barton 1930, 221–22]

Commencing with pregnancy and childbirth, basketry items traditionally play an indispensable role in numerous life-crisis ceremonies on the Cordillera. Among the Tinguian, ceremonial offerings are made before a pregnant woman's delivery. A family gathering is organized about a month before the anticipated birth, and the expectant mother partakes of a ritual meal of chicken while her relatives look on. After completing the meal, she places two bundles of grass, some bark, and beads in a small basket that she ties beside a window. Cole (1922, 262) reports that the significance of this act was no longer clear to the participants, who simply explained that it was "an old custom, and is pleasing to the spirits." After the delivery, a miniature basketry shield ensemble called *aneb* is placed above the newborn infant for spiritual protection (Cole 1922, 315–58; Capistrano-Baker 1995, 61).

Other basketry items will figure prominently in the course of the child's life. Boys will learn to make twined and plaited fish traps and other basketry objects essential to daily living. Girls in societies where basketmaking is not restricted to men will similarly learn to manufacture baskets, textiles, and pottery. As young men and women, they will participate in numerous rituals associated with agriculture, warfare and hunting, engagement and marriage, illness and death. Various baskets will be used in these ceremonies as ritual containers for offerings of rice, meat, rice beer, and sacrificial animals.

Answering both practical and spiritual needs, Cordillera baskets fulfill multiple functions throughout the life cycle, providing both temporal and divine protection, containing nourishment, sustaining life.

CHAPTER 2

Baskets among the Tanulong and Fidelisan Peoples of Northern Sagada

Albert S. Bacdayan

Casual observations suggest that among the peoples of the northern Luzon highlands,[1] baskets are perceived as utilitarian objects made for use in the course of daily existence. As such, they are perhaps more valued for their functionality than for any expression of creativity and beauty. Baskets are not, therefore, regarded as works of art, despite the fact that some of them may have artistic merit. And, with some exceptions, such as the sacred *takba*, which will be discussed later, neither are they religious objects valued for their symbolic or magical power.

It is because of their usefulness that baskets are ubiquitous. They are found in one form or another wherever people work in the fields, engage in activities at home in the villages, or travel from place to place. For this reason also, baskets are vulnerable to substitution or displacement by analogous objects from the outside world or to abandonment when and if they become obsolete in the changing environment.

ETHNOGRAPHIC CASE IN POINT

The use of and attitudes maintained toward basketry by the Fidelisan and Tanulong peoples of northern Sagada Municipality in the present Mountain Province confirm the foregoing impressions. The Fidelisan and Tanulong peoples see and consider themselves to be distinct groups despite the fact that they are very similar socially and culturally. In fact the area in which they differ most strikingly is their manner of speaking completely mutually understandable dialects, which are closely related to both the Bontoc and Kankanay languages. More specific to our purpose, the two groups are very similar in their utilitarian attitude toward basketry and the kinds of baskets they weave and use.[2]

FIGURE 2.1
A major use for the woman's transport basket known as the *labba* is carrying the rice harvest home. Women routinely carry huge loads on their heads at this time, while men use a *gimata* carried over their shoulders. This woman's empty *tupil*, or lunch box, hangs from the top of her load. Bangaan, Fidelisan, 1972.

Considered to be mainly western Bontoc culturally (Bacdayan 1974), the Fidelisan and Tanulong inhabit contiguous territories. They live in settlements extending from close to the Mabileng River, which flows through the lower and eastern portions of their territories on its way to join the well-known Chico River, up the western slope of the valley (fig. 2.2). Oral history has it that Pedlisan and Tanowong, from which the modern official designations Fidelisan and Tanulong are derived,[3] are the original villages. Each is less than a kilometer from the river. Several factors contributed to the flight from these

FIGURE 2.2
Fidelisan and Tanulong occupy a particularly rugged landscape of canyons and mountains in northwestern Mountain Province. This photograph, taken in 1972, shows the terraced rice fields of Fidelisan looking north.

FIGURE 2.3
Seedbeds for rice are often planted close to the village, as here on the outskirts of Tanulong in 1972. The seedlings are pulled and loaded into a *gimata* carrying basket, which is visible braced over the edge of a dike. They will be transplanted in distant fields.

original villages, among them the need to escape the ravages of epidemics and the raids of enemy groups during the era of headhunting. For those who responded positively to the efforts of Christian missionaries,[4] which commenced at the turn of the century, the perceived constraints of the traditional religious system provided further impetus for departure. Together, these developments led to the settlement of the villages of today (Bacdayan 1970).[5]

The economy and the rhythm of life of both groups traditionally centered on the cultivation of sweet potatoes, or camotes, and especially of rice (fig. 2.3). Legumes, corn, millet, squashes, and other vegetables are also grown, but rice and sweet potatoes are the main staples. The former, which takes up to eight months to mature and often yields sparse grain, is raised on laboriously and painstakingly built terraced fields literally carved out of mountainsides and land otherwise unsuitable for growing wet rice. These are irrigated by nearby springs or by water conveyed through gravity-fed ditches from sources often a considerable distance away (Bacdayan 1974). The construction and maintenance of the terraces and the irrigation works, as well as the actual cultivation of rice in the fields, are constant preoccupations. In contrast, sweet potatoes, which until recently constituted the main staple, do well in the cool and rugged highlands and are raised in upland dry fields. These do not require irrigation and elaborate terracing. Both rice terraces and camote fields are normally in the vicinity of the villages, for the most part a walk of a few minutes to two hours away.

As it is for the other inhabitants of the Cordillera, rice is the preferred food among the Fidelisan and Tanulong. Sweet potatoes are considered the food of last resort. Arising from the high value put on rice in the culture and the difficulty and unpredictability of raising it successfully, many religious customs and rituals are associated with its cultivation—from the sowing of the seedbeds in September to the harvest season in July (Bacdayan 1995). These include watchfulness for omens, rest days called *obaya*, and village welfare rituals called *begnas*.

The traditional religious system common to both the Fidelisan and Tanulong may be described as spirit worship. The spirits, called *anito*, include the dead and natural objects, such as mountains, bodies of water, rocks, and trees; thus the religion combines ancestor and nature worship. The living must maintain harmonious relations with the spirits just as they must maintain harmonious relations with each other. If the living neglect or in any way offend the spirits, they may encounter bad luck or become ill. The essence of worship, therefore, takes the form of propitiation and remembrance. Specific sacrificial rituals might entail the gathering of the kinship group to partake of a meal during which an offended spirit, named by a medium, is appealed to and remembered. The spirits, especially those of dead kinsmen, are also named and invited to come and partake of a meal during myriad social occasions, such as weddings. At such times, the dead ancestors are given a discreet period of time to eat, while the living, who will eat later, maintain silence. There are also villagewide aspects of this religious system centered in the men's houses.

FIGURE 2.4
Men lounge in the primary men's house (*dap-ay*), named Todey, at Fidelisan, 1972. A backpack-style basket (*sangi*) and spears have been left outside the entrance to the stone lounging platform.

FIGURE 2.5
Two Fidelisan men stand near a sacrificial post at the men's house (*dap-ay*). The man on the left wears the basketry hat known as *kinaw-it*, while the one on the right wears a *binekyeng*. A *tupil*, a basket used for carrying food to the fields, hangs on the post. 1972.

The Fidelisan and Tanulong villages are divided into wards, each of which has a men's house called *dap-ay* (figs. 2.4, 2.5). A ward may consist of ten to forty households, and there may be one or more wards in a village depending on its size. There is much coordination between the various men's houses; they cooperate with each other very closely, much like army units, for the good of the village. The men's houses are the educational, political, and religious centers of village life. Boys from age six or seven will sleep in the men's house until they are married. Each *dap-ay* has a common bed of rough-hewn boards in an enclosed building. A sunken circular courtyard contains a fireplace in the middle, which is surrounded by flat stones for lounging. The old men go to the *dap-ay* in the evenings to mingle with the young and to have them perform chores, such as massaging their legs or scratching the soles of their feet. In exchange, the elders tell stories and instruct the boys in village lore, tradition, and history. It is also in the *dap-ay* that the men meet and make decisions of villagewide import. Many of these decisions are religious in nature and have to do with rice cultivation, for example, determining when to observe *obaya*, or rest days, and when to perform the community welfare rituals, called *begnas* (fig. 2.6). On rest days, no work in the fields is allowed, although some labor may be done in the village, such as pounding rice and repairing or weaving baskets, provided that little noise is made. During the *begnas*, many rituals are performed in the men's houses. These include mock headhunting expeditions, during which the men of each *dap-ay* team up and depart the village brandishing spears and shields to look for omens; the performance of animal sacrifice under the village sacred tree; a communal meal; and sometimes dancing on the premises of the *dap-ay*.

Marriage is strictly monogamous, and the household is normally the nuclear family, although sometimes aged parents, especially the widowed, live with the family of one of their children. The nuclear family is the basic unit in the kinship system, which is bilateral of the so-called Eskimo type (Murdock 1960, 226-28).[6] The outer limit of the kinship group is thus the third cousin degree of relationship, reckoned equally from both sides of one's parentage. Roughly, all the ascendants and descendants of those within this limit, except the descendants of the third cousins, are members of the kinship group. This group is solidified by the many socioreligious affairs to which its members are invited. These occasions range in complexity. Simple episodic affairs include sacrificial ceremonies entailing the killing and eating of a chicken to cure illness and calendrical ceremonies to celebrate the end of the harvest season to which only siblings and their families are invited. More involved affairs entail the killing of at least a pig and two or more chickens. All-encompassing events, such as marriage celebrations, require the involvement of the entire breadth of the kinship group, including even the descendants of third cousins. Within the typical kinship group, there are numerous gatherings within the range from simple to all-encompassing in the course of a typical year.

FIGURE 2.6
Village ritual and social life revolves around the cycle of rice cultivation. Here, dancing takes place during a *begnas*, a community welfare ritual performed at the village's men's house (*dap-ay*) after rice planting is completed. Some gongs used for dancing are heirlooms made of Chinese bronze. Dap-ay Todey, Fidelisan, 1972.

A Dictionary of Fidelisan and Tanulong Baskets

Baskets are pervasive in the sociocultural setting just described. They are functional in the economic, social, and religious life of the Fidelisan and Tanulong peoples. The dictionary of basket types that follows gives evidence of their many functions.

Aggawin

The *aggawin* is a woman's work basket worn during all phases of rice cultivation. It hangs from the lower back by means of a cord tied around the hips. It is used for collecting fish, shells, and birds' eggs found while working, especially at harvest time, and for carrying a harvesting knife and split bamboo for bundling cut rice (fig. 2.7). It may also serve to carry tobacco, matches, and a pipe, although these are most often secured in the strands of beads that customarily hold a woman's hair in place. The *aggawin* is normally used only in connection with rice cultivation; it is not used when working in sweet potato fields mainly because there are no extraneous edibles, such as snails, birds' eggs, and fish, to be gathered.

FIGURE 2.7
A woman carries an *aggawin* on her hip while harvesting rice. Bansa, Tanulong, 1965.

Akiyak/akgi

The *akiyak* or *akgi* is a sievelike, loosely woven basket used by women to collect fish, tadpoles, and snails in the rice fields. Among the Tanulong, after the rice seeds have been sown in September, young women collect fish to make a delicacy called *linapet*, which they distribute to the young men in the village. The young men contribute to this effort, which has potential romantic significance, by providing the fatty meat that they are given by those in their ward who butcher pigs. The meat is their reward for maintaining the men's house (*dap-ay*) and especially for supplying it with firewood.

Akub

The *akub* is a large *tupil* used primarily for carrying cooked food for a large group working in the fields. Since most of the work involving large groups has to do with the cultivation of rice, the *akub* is most often used in the rice fields during harvesting, planting, and preparation for planting. At home, the *akub* may be used to store any number of items, such as rice and cooked food, especially meat.

Balikeng

The *balikeng* is a plaited basket that is square at the base and round at the top. It is scored and strengthened by a rim made of a combination of flat bamboo strips and rattan. The base is likewise scored and strengthened by a strip of wood that is lashed to it. The *balikeng* is used as a container for all sorts of foodstuffs, including sweet potatoes, rice, and vegetables. It is not used for long distance carrying on the head because the base is flexible and not sufficiently strong. It is not as widespread in households as the *labba* (see below) and is often purchased from other villages.

Ballaka

The *ballaka* is a sort of mound-shaped wicker hat that covers the back of the head and part of the crown. It is secured by a string looped across the forehead just below the hairline. It is used for personal adornment, as well as for carrying tobacco, matches, and a pipe. One version of the *ballaka* is narrower and more shallow; it is twined rather than made of wicker and is decorated by colored elements (black, yellow, and red) and strips of red trim at the side. This variant is said to be for young unmarried men, although one often sees married and older men wearing it. Both kinds of *ballaka* are decorated at the sides with a couple of boars' tusks (fig. 2.8). The wicker *ballaka* is typically worn by Fidelisan males and woven locally. The decorated type is imported from villages such as Guinaang and Maligcong to the east, close to Bontoc.

Ballokaw

The *ballokaw* is a carrying basket consisting of two round, loosely plaited baskets lashed to opposite ends of a pole. The pole is then placed across the shoulders. The *ballokaw* is used traditionally for transporting sweet potatoes and is now also employed to carry vegetables such as cabbages and peppers. This basket resembles the *gimata* but is more loosely woven.

FIGURE 2.8
Two types of *ballaka* may be seen here. The example on the left is made with the wicker technique (a variant of plaiting), while the example on the right uses the twining technique.

FIGURE 2.9
Old Man Bomatnong wears a *binekyeng* hat at his men's house (*dap-ay*). Cadatayan, Tanulong, 1972.

Binekyeng

The *binekyeng* is a coiled basketry hat for men (fig. 2.9). It has a raised circular center that is flat at the top and to which long rooster tail feathers are attached as decoration. Like the *ballaka*, it is also used for carrying matches, tobacco, and a pipe, as well as small portions of meat that the wearer may be given at various social occasions. This type of hat is typical of Sagada to the south but is also worn by some men in both Tanulong and Fidelisan. Among the Sagada people, the *binekyeng* can only be worn by men who have celebrated the marriages of their children with a feast called *dawak* or *bayas* and who are not faced with ritual impediments due to misbehavior, such as adultery, or to unfortunate events in the family, such as the death of a marriageable son or daughter. Hence, wearing the *binekyeng* is a sign of acceptability to one's peers or of good moral standing. Men who use the hat without meeting the requirements are scorned.

Bitoto

A small plaited basket, the *bitoto* is square at the base and round at the top. It is normally between 9 and 12 inches in diameter. The *bitoto* is a general purpose container used for newly pound rice, sweet potatoes, and vegetables. It is not used for transporting burdens.

Dugong

The *dugong* is a box-shaped cage for housing hens and their chicks at night (fig. 2.10). Every family has at least one *dugong* because chickens and pigs are the main sacrificial animals in the local religion. It is therefore a cultural expectation that each household will have one or more pigs and some chickens at all times.

FIGURE 2.10
Old Woman Maliked dries unhusked rice in her yard, using a winnowing tray (*liga-u*). To the right and left are chicken houses (*dugong*) for keeping mother hens and chicks safe at night. Cadatayan, Tanulong, 1972.

Ekab

A wicker basket, narrower at the bottom than at the top, the *ekab* was used traditionally for containing and transporting locusts. Early in the twentieth century, however, locust swarms ceased to be a problem, and, as a result these baskets are rarely seen today. They have largely deteriorated and disintegrated due to neglect.

FIGURE 2.11
A man wearing a hat known as *kinaw-it* carries an empty *gimata* on his way to the fields. Madongo, Tanulong, 1972.

Gimata

The *gimata* is a plaited transport basket. One *gimata* is fastened to each end of a pole, which is then carried across the shoulders. This basket is used primarily for transporting rice, but it is also used for carrying other items, such as sweet potatoes (fig. 2.11). During the wedding season (December to February and June to August) when large animals, such as cows and water buffalo, are butchered on the outskirts of the villages, the *gimata* is used to transport meat. It can even be used to carry manure. This is the primary transport basket among both Fidelisan and Tanulong. Each family has at least one *gimata*.

Giyag

A plaited food tray, the *giyag* is used for serving rice or sweet potatoes. During mealtimes the *giyag* functions as a common tray for use by two or more people who reach for the food with their hands. Each family has several *giyag*. The fact that this tray is used for serving food in the manner described may have been the idea behind the practice called *kiyag* (*giyag*) among the central Bontoc. This is a formalized food exchange between families or kin groups at a marriage. The food to be exchanged may in fact be conveyed in this type of tray. A *giyag* is illustrated in catalog number 13.

Kalaw

The *kalaw* is a loosely plaited cage for carrying chickens. Although it is very convenient, it is not commonly used. Most chickens taken to the fields for ritual ceremonies or transported anywhere for any purpose are often simply bound by the legs to prevent their escape and held by hand.

Kalikog

The *kalikog* is a small plaited basket, somewhat swaybacked in shape, with a protruding opening at each end that gives the impression of horns. It is used by girls for storing green rice and thus resembles the *kamkam-u* used by boys. The *kalikog* is also called *tuklobaw*.

Kamkam-u

The *kamkam-u* is a miniature *kamuwan* (see below) used by children to store sweetened green rice, which is considered a treat during harvest time. Like the *kalikog* (see above), it is also called *tuklobaw*. Green rice, known as *do-om*, is a treat much anticipated by young and old alike during harvest time. The harvesting party traditionally cuts a few bundles of rice that have not yet ripened (there is always some unripe rice in the field). At home in the village at the end of the day, the green rice is separated from the straw and partly roasted. It is then pounded. The resulting tender green rice is sweetened with brown sugar, the children's *tuklobaw* are filled, and the treat is consumed with much delight.

FIGURE 2.12
Old Man Bomatnong leads a work party to clean Tanulong's 18-kilometer, gravity fed irrigation canal. On this occasion he wears the more informal *kinaw-it* hat (compare fig. 2.9). His earlobes are distended from the use of locally fashioned gold earrings, and his pipe is tucked under the strap of his hat. 1972.

Kamuwan

The *kamuwan* is a plaited basket with a lid for storing husked rice that is ready for cooking. It is comparable to the basket illustrated as catalog number 6.

Kinaw-it

The *kinaw-it* is a coiled man's basketry hat (fig. 2.12). It is typical of the Tanulong, although it is also used by Fidelisan men. It is smaller but deeper than the *ballaka* and covers only the back of the crown. Like the *ballaka*, it is used as a "pocket" for carrying matches, tobacco, and pipes and is secured to the head by means of a string anchored within the hairline or carried across the forehead.

Labba/lowa

A woman's transport basket with a plaited square bottom and circular top, the *labba*, or *lowa*, has twined or sometimes wickerwork sides. It sits on top of the head and is used for carrying any burden from light items to heavy goods such as rice or sweet potatoes (figs. 2.13, 2.1). Lined with banana leaves, it may also be used during large gatherings as a serving container for cooked rice and meat. When large animals, especially pigs, are butchered at ritual and celebratory occasions, the intestines are put in the *labba* for the women waiting nearby to clean.

FIGURE 2.13
Among a group going to a wedding, one woman carries her gift of bundles of rice in a *labba*. Aguid, Fidelisan, 1972.

Lablabba

A small version of the *labba*, the *lablabba* shares the same construction. It is a versatile domestic basket for use in carrying a variety of small burdens, such as vegetables, husked rice, and dried beans. It is often used instead of the *akub* for carrying lunch for work groups in the fields. Though important, it is not as crucial as the *labba*, or *lowa*.

Liga-u

The *liga-u* is a plaited, flat winnowing basket used to separate a husk or outer covering from a grain or berry, as with rice or coffee. It is very shallow, and a rim of bamboo and rattan lashed to the bottom constitutes the entire side. Its wide flat shape makes it ideal for drying legumes, coffee beans, or rice in the sun. It may, like the *labba*, also be used as a serving container for cooked food such as rice or meat. The *liga-u* is an essential household basket in rice-growing societies like Fidelisan and Tanulong (see fig. 2.10).

Oppigan/kuppit

The *oppigan*, or *kuppit*, is a special, finely plaited man's shoulder basket with two or three layered compartments. The bottom layer, the largest and main compartment, is usually used for carrying meat or other food; while the other sections contain tobacco, matches, and sometimes money. The *oppigan* is not an everyday basket. It is supposed to be used only by old men, specifically those who have successfully married off their children with the proper celebrations and who have grandchildren. These men use the *oppigan* for special occasions including meetings, assemblies, rituals, and celebrations. It is thus an indication of status. The *oppigan* is often imported from other mountain groups, such as the people in the municipality of Besao to the west. The *oppigan* is comparable to the basket illustrated in catalog number 50.

Pangitlogan

The name *pangitlogan* literally means a place for depositing or delivering eggs, in short, a nest. Thus the term refers to wickerwork baskets of varying shapes that are used as nests. Like the *dugong*, every family has at least one nest basket used for chickens. The baskets are kept tucked under the eaves of houses.

Pasiking

The *pasiking* is a plaited basket that is worn on the back and does not have a lid. It is woven totally of rattan. While it is not as popular as the *sangi*, it is used for carrying pretty much the same things. It can, however, accommodate bulkier and longer objects than the *sangi* because there is no lid. For this reason, it is said to be preferred by hunters.

FIGURE 2.14
A man on his way to perform a ritual at his rice field carries a *sangi* containing the necessary elements: cooked rice, salt pork, and a pot for cooking the meat. He also carries his spear and some dry pine branches for the fire. Tanulong, 1972.

Sallong/Sagada

The *sallong*, or *sagada*, is a loosely plaited basket used for trapping fish as they move from place to place. This basket has a round open top with a diameter of approximately 14 inches; it may have a narrow bottom. The *sallong* is not common because very little fishing is done.

Sangi

A plaited backpack with a lid, the *sangi* is normally used by men for carrying a wide variety of items—rice, meat, beans, lunch, tools, and even, on occasion, small children. It is said to have been used in the past by headhunters for carrying their trophies back to the home village. The *sangi* hangs from two braided shoulder straps, hugging the back. It is the most popular basket for men because it is so versatile. The *sangi* and *pasiking* are especially handy for carrying needed items when going on trips or to work (fig. 2.14). These two baskets are often imported from other groups, especially those to the east, who have easy access to rattan, the material from which they are woven.

Takba

The *takba* is a small plaited men's lunch basket carried on the back by means of shoulder straps. It is essentially an individual lunch basket, although some examples may be large enough to carry lunch for two. See also the separate section on the sacred *takba*, below.

Takodog

The *takodog* is a strong plaited basket resembling, but much larger and deeper than, the *bitoto*. It is used for bailing water out of a pool in which one is fishing. Like the *sallong*, or *sagada*, it is not a very common basket because river fishing is infrequently practiced.

Tinangban/Tambala

A finely made basket with a lid, the *tinangban*, or *tambala*, is used for carrying food. This may include meals to be eaten in the fields or gifts of rice and beans for relatives. This basket may also be used to store sewing and weaving materials. The *tinangban* has a plaited square base and a round top finished with a fine, carefully lashed, piece of wood that serves as the rim on which the lid fits. It is a valued basket because of its fine workmanship and thus tends to be used to carry a gift of rice on special occasions, such as weddings. This basket is often imported from the Agawa and other groups in neighboring Besao Municipality, as they are noted for weaving especially fine examples. A comparable basket is illustrated as catalog number 9.

Tupil

The *tupil* is a plaited basket with a lid that is used for carrying cooked food to the field. In addition to its usual function as a lunch basket, it is also used to transport food to be shared with those kinsmen who could not be present at a ritual occasion. The *tupil* is square at the base and the top (the base of the lid is square); but it narrows and rounds in the middle forming a "waist." It is strongly made with a strip of wood and rattan lashed to the base and emphasizing its square shape. Braided ribbing runs along the base of the lid (the top of the basket, in effect), and sometimes a strip of bamboo or wood appears across the middle of the basket. The lid is attached and secured by means of a cord emanating from two sides of the basket's base (see fig. 2.1).

Ube/Ugat

The *ube*, or *ugat*, is a mudfish trap. *Ube* are normally woven and used by boys, although men may also weave them for their children (fig. 2.15). *Ube* are employed to catch fish in the rice fields for about four months starting from the time the rice crop is harvested until the fields are turned over in preparation for planting. The traps are set in the evenings, gathered early the following morning, and brought home to dry for use again the next evening. A boy normally has thirty or more *ube*, and a version of this trap is used for catching tadpoles.

FIGURE 2.15
A young man plaits a fish trap, *ube*, beginning with the conical opening through which the fish will enter. Bangaan, Fidelisan, 1972.

The widespread use of the *ube* has been drastically curtailed among the Fidelisan people because the mudfish population was decimated by a fish of foreign origin, which was introduced by well-meaning agricultural extension workers as a supplementary source of protein. Unfortunately, the predator fish is small, bony, and generally disliked by the Fidelisan.

BASKETMAKING AND USE IN FIDELISAN AND TANULONG

In all, there are thirty baskets known and used by the Fidelisan and Tanulong Igorots. Six of these are primarily, if not completely, related to rice (*aggawin*, *kalikog*, *kamkam-u*, *kamuwan*, *liga-u*, and *gimata*); three are basically hats that also serve as containers (*ballaka*, *kinaw-it*, and *binekyeng*); four are associated with fishing (*sallong*, *takodog*, *ube*, and *akiyak*); three are related to chickens (*dugong*, *pangitlogan*, and *kalaw*); one (*ekab*) was traditionally used for collecting locusts and is today practically nonexistent; and the rest are everyday work and carrying baskets. As I have tried to make clear, not all the baskets are locally made. Many are produced by other groups and imported by the Fidelisan and Tanulong peoples. The fact that there are six baskets pertaining to rice is not at all surprising given that the production and consumption of this grain is a pronounced cultural focus. The number could in fact be increased to seven if we recall that the *akiyak* is used to catch fish for the *linapet* exchange—an event that occurs in the course of rice cultivation. It is interesting that there are four items having to do with fishing considering that not much fishing is done. Two of these, the *akiyak* and the *ube* are used solely in the rice fields, while the *sallong* and the *takodog* are used both in the rice fields and for river fishing.

Fidelisan and Tanulong baskets are woven from two kinds of bamboo, *bika* and *anes*, and from rattan. *Bika* abounds in the forests within the environs of Fidelisan and Tanulong villages, while rattan and *anes* are scarce resources found at least a day or more distant. Because some intergroup enmity exists, often dating back to headhunting days, local men are at some risk when they journey beyond their usual territorial range. As a result, rattan and *anes* are often imported from other villages. It is not unusual, especially in the case of rattan, to see men from neighboring groups with greater access loaded with quantities of this material to trade. Completed baskets woven from these relatively rare materials are also peddled.

Most woven baskets are plaited, although wickerwork, twining, and coiling are also practiced. As is common all over the world, a basket may involve several techniques—particularly wickerwork, twining, and plaiting—and it may also employ more than one material in its construction. The *labba* is a case in point. Its base is laid out by plaiting, and after the right width is woven, the plaited elements are bent upward. These are then used to form the spokes for twining or wickerwork until the right width and depth of the basket are attained. The ends of the elements are then securely tied, and the spokes are cut. A rim consisting of two or three rattan strips is lashed and securely fastened to the body of the basket. A rim of wood is likewise attached to the base and lashed with rattan.

Among the Fidelisan and Tanulong basket weaving is done by men. A man usually makes baskets as the need arises. As a result, there is no specialization, and no particular credit is given to the weaver, although his work may be noted and appreciated. This may in fact lead to requests that he make baskets for others. Farming chores, however, prevent basketmaking from becoming a full-time occupation. As already noted, many baskets used in the villages are imported. Most notable among these are the *tinangban* and *oppigan*, which are largely imported from Agawa and other villages in valleys to the west, and the *sangi* and the bachelor's *ballaka*, imported from villages in valleys to the east. The baskets typically woven in Fidelisan and Tanulong are the *kinaw-it*, *liga-u*, *labba*, *sallong*, *dugong*, *pangitlogan*, and *bitoto*. With the exception of the *liga-u*, these baskets tend to be manufactured locally because they are woven from the readily available *bika*.

An imaginary trip to one of the original villages, say Tanulong, will vividly reveal the ubiquity of baskets. Descending from Madongo, a mountaintop Tanulong village, we might encounter groups of people, usually families, on their way to work. The women carry *labba* on their heads, which contain, among other things, the *tupil* with their lunches and the *aggawin* that they will fasten around their hips as they work in the rice field. As a woman comes across a mudfish, snail, or bird's egg, she puts it in her *aggawin*. Others, including men, who do not have *aggawin* deposit their finds in the *aggawin* of a relative or friend. The men wear their basketry hats in which they store tobacco, matches, and pipes. Even if a man does not smoke, he puts on his *ballaka*, which is customary everyday wear. The men also have *sangi* on their backs. Inside these backpacks are any number of things, for example, additional food to eat in the field or a pot with meat, especially if the work party intends to perform a ritual in the field. During harvest time, the men carry their empty *gimata*, which they use to haul the rice harvest back to the village.

Down in the village, we see empty cages off to the side of the areas paved with stone in front of homes. These are *dugong*, the baskets used to keep hens and their chicks safe from predators at night. Elsewhere under the eaves fastened to the wall or posts are one or two *pangitlogan* in which the family's hens lay and hatch their eggs. Somewhere in front of the house might lie a *gimata*, a *labba*, an *akiyak*, or a *liga-u*. Invited inside the house, we see *giyag* leaning on their sides on a shelf above where the cooking pots are stored, near the family hearth at one side of the living space. In this storage area are also wooden bowls, wide wooden serving platters or trays, as well as other cooking equipment. In a narrow elevated space, called *lad-ey*, to one side of the living space and some distance from the hearth, is the *kamuwan* where threshed rice is stored and the *liga-u*, or winnowing tray, that is used to separate the rice from the husk. In the *lad-ey* we may also see a *tinangban*.

If our trip to Tanulong is to celebrate a wedding, we will doubtless see *giyag* for use during the meal and *labba* laden with cooked rice ready to be served. Men carry *oppigan*, or shoulder baskets, and sport hats—*ballaka* or *binekyeng* decorated with bright rooster tail feathers. Some men use *gimata* to carry meat from the place where water buffalo or cows have been slaughtered for the celebration. Many of the out-of-town guests wear *sangi* on their backs or carry gifts and contributions in *labba*. If our trip is made to attend a community welfare ceremony, or *begnas*, we will in all likelihood see baskets blackened with soot and decorated with feathers hanging from the post at the edge

FIGURE 2.16
A young man carries his family's sacred *takba* at the *kayew*, a major ritual of the rice growing cycle. Traditional and contemporary headgear coexist at all kinds of occasions. Angtin, Tanulong, 1972.

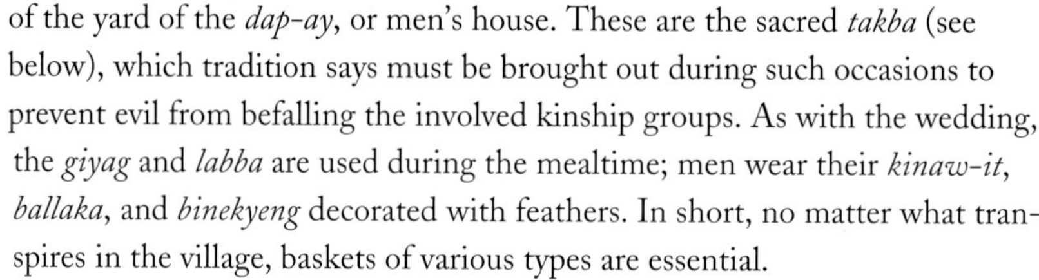

of the yard of the *dap-ay*, or men's house. These are the sacred *takba* (see below), which tradition says must be brought out during such occasions to prevent evil from befalling the involved kinship groups. As with the wedding, the *giyag* and *labba* are used during the mealtime; men wear their *kinaw-it*, *ballaka*, and *binekyeng* decorated with feathers. In short, no matter what transpires in the village, baskets of various types are essential.

THE SACRED TAKBA

Takba (fig. 2.16) is the name of the only religious or sacred basket in Fidelisan and Tanulong. Though called *takba*, this basket is, in fact, a *sangi* without a lid, and thus it bears no resemblance to the *takba* discussed earlier, which is a type of men's lunch basket. Sacred *takba* belong to an entire kinship group or to a number of related kinship groups and are said to memorialize victims of headhunting or those who have died unusual violent deaths, such as being struck by lightning. The *takba* is kept inside the home in a place warmed by the heat emanating from the hearth. On occasion, a *takba* is brought out by the head of the family that houses it. It is inspected for damage, and the salted meat and *tapuy*, or fermented rice in a bamboo tube, kept within it are replenished. As noted earlier, the village holds welfare feasts, or *begnas*, centered in the men's houses (fig. 2.17). These often involve the men leaving the village, as if they were on a headhunting expedition, to look for omens. On such occasions, the *takba* must be taken with the party (fig. 2.18). For the duration of welfare feasts that are centered in the village, however, the *takba* are hung from a post near the paved lounging area surrounding the fireplace of the men's house.

FIGURE 2.17
Families are obligated to bring their sacred *takba* to the *dap-ay* to be displayed at the *begnas* rites. Failure to do so is believed to result in dire consequences for the family concerned. While sacred *takba* may be of various shapes, they all have a shiny black patina from smoke and soot, because they are kept in the home above or near the open hearth. Dap-ay Nabaneng, Cadatayan, Tanulong, 1972.

To neglect the *takba* is to risk dire consequences in the form of physical and, especially, mental illness; the *takba* is generally thought to be responsible for any abnormal behavior. When this occurs, the kinship group is mobilized to contribute time and especially money to sponsor a *begnas*. The group concerned provides the animals (chickens and pigs) to be sacrificed and eaten. All these events focus attention and sympathy on the afflicted while at the same

FIGURE 2.18
A group of Tanulong men rests on the way home from an overnight mock headhunting encampment during the 1972 ritual cycle. The sacred *takba* appears at lower left. The spears too are now heirlooms, the significance of which is tied to the ways of the past.

time solidifying the kinship group and the village. No wonder then that they often have beneficial effects.

What to do with the *takba* is a dilemma for family groups in Fidelisan and Tanulong who have been acculturated, follow modern values, and take Christianity seriously. Although they often come to ignore the *takba*, regarding it as pagan and old-fashioned, Christian and acculturated families have nonetheless been forced to perform *takba*-related rituals or assist with them by contributing money for use in curing the affliction of somebody in the family or in the kinship group back in the village. If the afflicted lives outside the home village, he or she must be brought back for such rituals.

DISPLACEMENT, ABANDONMENT, AND SURVIVAL

Sadly, since the late 1950s baskets have become less and less apparent in the day-to-day life of the Fidelisan and Tanulong. They have been gradually displaced by store-bought substitutes. The *giyag* is giving way to modern enameled tin and aluminum plates and trays; the *tupil* and *akub* find successors in Tupperware-type containers and lunch boxes; the *sangi* and *pasiking* are supplanted by cloth and canvas backpacks; the *kamuwan*, *kamkam-u*, and *kalikog* are replaced with tin cans; and the heirs of *ballaka*, *kinaw-it*, and *binekyeng* seem to be purchased caps and hats (fig. 2.19), to give only a few examples. That this displacement has been accomplished so easily seems to be a function of the utilitarian nature of the traditional baskets—valued for their usefulness rather than as art or religious objects. If plastic, aluminum, and enameled containers can serve the same purpose as traditional baskets, and these replace-

FIGURE 2.19
Many traditional basketry items are now being replaced with imported industrial goods. The first of these two men shown entering a home wears a *kinaw-it* basketry hat, while the second wears a miner's hat known locally as "hard-boiled." Tanulong, 1972.

ments are affordable, easy to obtain, and regarded as superior or more practical, then they are adopted. It is conceivable, therefore, that traditional baskets, with the exception of the sacred *takba*, may one day soon be things of the past to be seen only in museums, and then mostly in America.

As a result of changes that are taking place in the manner of harvesting, even the distinctive *gimata* may one day lose its preeminence as the basket of choice for carrying rice. Traditionally, rice panicles are cut one-by-one from the stalk, which is held by the stem in one hand. They are carefully bundled in quantities that can be measured in a circle formed by the forefinger and the thumb. These bundles, called *benge*, are cultural units of quantity by means of which the productivity of a rice field is measured. The *benge* are packed in either the *gimata* or on the *labba* and carried home to the village. Now, however, some Tanulong and Fidelisan are harvesting without bundling, a faster process. The panicles are cut by the handful, stuffed in sacks, and then carried home. As the local people become increasingly cash oriented, they tend to raise vegetables in the terraced fields instead of rice; and the *ballokaw* is better suited for carrying such crops. If this trend continues, the *gimata* may go the way of the *ekab*, the locust basket now abandoned because it is no longer useful in the environment.

Among the Fidelisan and Tanulong, the sacred *takba* is in a category all by itself. In Durkheim's terms, the memorial *takba* belongs to the realm of the sacred, while other baskets in Fidelisan and Tanulong appear to exist in the realm of the profane.[7] The chances of it disappearing quietly like the *ekab* or being displaced by a substitute are not likely. This is because its function is psychological and spiritual, based on belief. While the sacred *takba* may be a memorial basket for someone who existed in the past, it has acquired a life or existence all its own. It is believed to have power if neglected, and this power is punitive. It is likely, therefore, that the sacred *takba* will persist for some time to come, at least as long as its neglect is believed to cause misfortune.

Ironically, the potential for survival of selected traditional baskets from the northern Luzon high country resides in tourism. A growing interest in the Philippines and in the world at large regarding things "native" or original coupled with what may be called ethnic pride and cultural nationalism on the part of the Igorot themselves may have positive effects. This is already evident in the case of the *sangi*, or back basket. It is not unusual these days to see educated highlanders, who might have preferred a store-bought backpack, traveling to cities in the mountain region and in the lowlands, such as Baguio and Manila, wearing the *sangi*. And in Baguio—the educational center of the highland region—a thin, small version of the *sangi* appears to be a favorite book bag of highland and lowland college students alike. Finally, as tourists pour into the area, they want local artifacts including baskets as mementos. These factors combine to create a demand ensuring the survival of some of the traditional baskets.

CHAPTER 3

Making and Marketing Contemporary Baskets in Ifugao Province, Northern Luzon

B. Lynne Milgram

FIGURE 3.1
A basket maker uses an awl in basket construction. Banaue, 1995.

INTRODUCTION

Frank Alindayo, thirty-six and a small Ifugao landowner, began helping his father make baskets when he was twelve years old.[1] He first learned how to clean the bamboo and rattan to prepare it for basketmaking. On weekends and during holidays when he was not attending school, Frank practiced the basic plaiting technique by making the small baskets that neighbors ordered. He is now skilled in making a variety of baskets that are always in demand to hold cooked food (e.g., rice and sweet potatoes) and carry crops from the fields. Albert Tayad, forty-two, does not own land. For much of his income, he thus depends on his family's long tradition of making the baskets required for both daily and ritual use. Since the mid-1970s, however, the increasing number of tourists coming to view the region's rice terraces has prompted Albert to increase his share of this emerging market. Using traditional construction techniques, Albert has started to design new basketry forms such as small sweet potato trays to meet consumers' tastes and their demand for an "indigenous" memento from Ifugao.

As the above accounts suggest, in Banaue, Ifugao Province, northern Luzon, basketmaking continues as a vibrant art form. Artisans, both men and women, fashion a variety of baskets for daily use, for special ceremonial occasions, and for sale to tourists. Indeed, the commoditization of the local, agrarian economy and the increasing number of Western and lowland Filipino tourists coming to view Banaue's spectacular rice terraces have contributed to a tourist market for contemporary crafts. Selling crafts such as baskets to tourists has emerged as the most viable way for Banaue farmers to earn additional cash to secure the livelihoods of their households. Income from craft production provides the cash the family will need to purchase basic household necessities for much of the year. However, while the small but steady domestic demand for baskets keeps artisans producing throughout the year on an as-needed basis, the larger commercial demand for crafts is subject to the seasonal boom-and-bust cycle of the tourist industry. The fluctuations in the tourist market have meant that artisans cannot afford to abandon their dependence on agriculture. Rather, artisan-cultivators combine basket production with other income-generating activities to meet their subsistence needs.

In this chapter, the production of baskets in Banaue, Ifugao Province, serves as a case study of the economic and cultural importance of craft production for rural households. I describe the different types of baskets currently made, the conditions of their manufacture, and how baskets communicate their meaning through their use in different situations. What makes contemporary basketmaking in Banaue so noteworthy is that despite increasing tourism and commoditization of the rural economy, current production has not caved in to tourists' demands. Artisans continue to produce baskets for everyday and ritual use. This "traditional" production coexists with commercial production designed specifically for sale to local Banaue and regional Baguio City tourist markets. Artisans engage in both spheres of basketmaking simultaneously. In so doing, they bridge the gap between the requirements of their indigenous customs and the demands of new consumer tastes. This study thus demonstrates how artisans maintain control of craft production and exchange processes to more firmly secure their household income and to determine the nature of their involvement in the world market system.

THE SETTING: BANAUE, IFUGAO PROVINCE, NORTHERN LUZON, PHILIPPINES

The Ifugao live on the eastern side of the Gran Cordillera Central, the mountain range that extends through northern Luzon. This essay focuses on the villages in the municipality of Banaue that are known for their basket production (e.g., Cambulo, Pula, Tam-an, Bocos, Amganad). In these villages, an average of 55 percent of each of the villages' approximately 250 households, have at least one member involved in craft production or trade (e.g., basketmaking, weaving, wood carving). The main economic activity in Banaue, as throughout the Cordillera, is subsistence wet-rice cultivation, as described by Florina Capistrano-Baker in her introductory essay. Cultivating rice in irrigated paddies, or pond fields, is carried out on narrow fields that terrace the region's

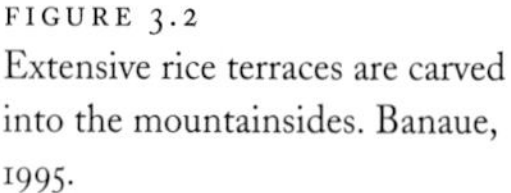

FIGURE 3.2
Extensive rice terraces are carved into the mountainsides. Banaue, 1995.

steep mountain landscape (fig. 3.2). Rice cultivation skills are respected because of the time, knowledge, and labor required to secure a good harvest.

Rice is the preferred subsistence crop in Ifugao as throughout the Philippines. Banaue's high elevation, 1,500 meters, and cool climate, however, limit cultivation to just one rice crop per year. This restriction of one yearly planting means that only the wealthiest Ifugao can eat rice year round. The staple food for most people is the camote, or sweet potato, grown in swiddens, or slash-and-burn hillside gardens. Swidden farming, however, is not as prestigious as rice cultivation, and although the camote is easier to grow, it is relegated to second place, below that of rice. Early twentieth-century anthropologist Roy Barton (1919; see also Conklin 1980; Bacdayan 1995) confirms that during his time in Ifugao, the primary indicator of a family's wealth and prestige was ownership of irrigated land and whether or not the family had enough "native" upland rice to serve at meals year round. Any surplus of upland rice is still never sold but rather stored for later distribution to family and community members on special ritual occasions to enhance the cultural prestige of the giver. Thus, many families must augment their income with cash-earning activities such as craft production. In other agricultural activities, women grow vegetables for household needs and raise pigs and chickens.

Currently, however, wealth is also measured by the amount of cash one has been able to accumulate, often from successful businesses such as handicrafts or running a dry goods store. Amassed capital may be transformed, in turn, into other traditional signs of Ifugao status such as sponsorship of local community rituals and feasts. The newly rich are identified as *bacnang*[2] rather than as *kadangyan*, which signifies the landed elite. *Bacnang*, however, can continue to earn prestige and respect within the community by following culturally prescribed customs such as the sponsorship of these ritual feasts.

The people of the Gran Cordillera Central resisted Spanish domination for three hundred years (1565–1898). Their region became part of the Philippine state through negotiation rather than conquest during the American colonial period, 1898–1946. Early American policy in this region stressed local control over local economy and resources. Although this policy was later reversed, it set the precedent for the autonomy of the indigenous population (Jenista 1987). This has meant that many of the community's cultural and economic elements have remained dynamic and provide the basis of unique local development. For example, the production of crafts by independent artisans coexists with a commercial market economy that was introduced in the early 1900s and accelerated after the Second World War, and particularly since the 1970s with growing tourism. Similarly, traditional Ifugao animism and belief in an ancestral cult coexist in a setting where, from 1900 and increasingly since the 1950s, most Ifugao have been baptized as Roman Catholic. The pluralism of Banaue's socioeconomic practices provides a provocative context within which to situate the dynamics of craft production, such as basketmaking, at the household level.

CONTEMPORARY BASKET PRODUCTION IN BANAUE: ARTISANS, MATERIALS, AND TECHNOLOGY

In Banaue, as throughout Ifugao, baskets are made primarily by men within the context of a household industry. Artisans work in their homes and may be assisted by their spouses and children who help with the preliminary cleaning and scraping of the rattan and bamboo (fig. 3.3).[3] Men of all ages make baskets, but not all men are basket makers. For the most part, basketmaking is a part-time endeavor to be balanced with agricultural work, wage work, and domestic responsibilities, which men share with their wives. In most cases men learn basketry skills from male family members (fathers, cousins, or uncles). Equipment requirements are minimal, and artisans work individually in their homes.

While some basket makers specialize in particular items, most possess the skills to construct different kinds of basket products depending upon the demand. Some of the types of baskets commonly produced in Ifugao today for both everyday and ceremonial use are included in the catalog. These include the backpack, or *hapē'eng* (cat. no. 25); the chicken coop, or *ubi* (cat. no. 31); the winnowing tray, or *liga-u* (cat. no. 2); the fish trap, or *gūbu* (cat. no. 38); and different types of food baskets (e.g., *hū'up*, *balyag*, *allataw*, *tudung*) used to hold cooked food or carry harvested crops (e.g., rice or sweet potatoes) from the field to the house (cat. nos. 8, 18, 19, 42).

How do basket makers in Banaue obtain the materials they need to construct their baskets? Artisans follow two channels to gain access to supplies of raw materials. Baskets are made primarily from bamboo and rattan. Up until approximately fifteen years ago, supplies of both of these materials were locally available in the well-forested areas of Ifugao Province. However, with deforestation and with no ongoing plan to renew reserves of natural resources, local supplies of bamboo and rattan have been seriously depleted. Artisans must now travel further into the forests of neighboring regions to secure the raw materials they require. Basket makers in the villages of Cambulo and Pula, for example, often make the long walk to Barlig in neighboring Mountain Province to secure their supplies. At the same time as local supplies of rattan and bamboo are decreasing, increasing supplies of these materials are required to fulfill the growing demands of local and regional tourist markets. In response to these demands, itinerant vendors from lowland provinces, such as Nueva Vizcaya, have started to sell rattan and bamboo at Banaue's Saturday market. Each week three or four women bring large coils of basketmaking materials from provinces south of Ifugao to sell to local artisans by the kilo. Materials that are not sold are left on consignment with local craft shop owners. In 1995 rattan and bamboo sold for 70 to 80 pesos (U.S. $3.00) per kilo. Paying for materials once free and locally available adds to the artisans' basic costs of production. Hence, basket makers are constantly negotiating with their main buyers, local Banaue craft shop owners and independent traders, to secure higher prices for their products in order to offset the added expense of purchasing materials.

FIGURE 3.3
Artisan cleaning rattan in preparation for basketmaking. Banaue, 1995.

Indeed, some of the craft shop owners who sell baskets have started to make regular trips to lowland provinces to buy basketmaking supplies. Artisans who cannot afford to buy their own raw materials either obtain supplies of bamboo and rattan from craft shop owners in the form of an in-kind loan or accept advances of these supplies in a piecework arrangement. In the former instance, the cost of the materials is later deducted from the value of the baskets that artisans subsequently bring to the shop owner to sell.[4] In the latter instance, artisans work on a per item basis in which they are paid only for their labor. Neither system, however, is hegemonic. Basket makers decide in which system of production to participate depending upon their resources and their ability to continue their tradition of individual home production.[5]

Artisans use simple hand tools to produce baskets. A small curved knife is used to clean and scrape the outer layers of the rattan and bamboo and split the pieces into the appropriate thickness in preparation for basketmaking (see fig. 3.3). A metal awl is also used. The awl allows the basket maker to separate sections of the plaiting in order to insert new pieces or to adjust the spacing (fig. 3.1). Plaiting is the main construction technique used by men to make baskets.

In Banaue the persistence of artisan-controlled techniques of basket construction means that the technology of basketmaking remains largely "holistic" (Franklin 1992, 18). In a holistic technology Franklin (1992, 18) explains, artisans control the process of their own work from beginning to end. Using holistic methods does not mean that people do not work together, but the manner in which this work is done "leaves the individual worker in control of a particular process of creating or doing something" (Franklin 1992, 19). Artisans are responsible for the preparation of the materials and for the actual construction of the basket. Franklin regards technology as "social practice," its meaning firmly rooted in particular contexts (1992, 15). By applying her concept of holistic technology to Banaue's basketmaking, it becomes evident that in each stage of production producers make situational decisions regarding the basket's construction. They draw on their own experience, each time applying it to a slightly different situation. Although the products of their work may appear identical to the casual observer, particularly in the case of traditional pieces, each basket demonstrates the hand and control of the maker.

How then do artisans integrate basketmaking with their agricultural responsibilities to secure the livelihoods of their households? Artisans make functional baskets throughout the year in response to demands from community members. Baskets destined for the local tourist shops in Banaue and for the regional tourist markets in Baguio City, the regional administrative center, are made primarily in December and between February and May when the warm, dry weather signals the height of the tourist season. Ultimately, however, artisans' engagement in basket production is tempered by the need for their labor in rice cultivation. During December and January, for example, women are busy planting and transplanting the rice seedlings, while men use this time to repair rice terrace walls and pathways. As it is still cool and often rains in Banaue at this time, the few tourists visiting the region provide only a medium-level demand for local crafts. During these months, basket makers decide how to divide their time between crafts and cultivation to maximize their earnings; they shift their labor between these two activities to fill the orders of local community members and the small demand from tourists. From June through August, however, artisans prefer to participate in the harvest. This community activity renews family and neighborhood ties and offers participants opportunities to earn their own local upland rice, supplies of which are culturally, as well as materially, valued. Because this is also the rainy season, there are few tourists visiting Banaue. Hence, there is little incentive to produce baskets for other-than-local needs during this time.

The following case study illustrates how one artisan combines different basketry activities with his agricultural responsibilities to secure his household's subsistence needs. Pedro Bannug, forty-seven, contributes to the support of his wife and five children with his earnings from basketmaking. He sells his baskets to one particular craft shop owner in the Banaue market with whom he has developed a patron-client, or *suki*, relationship. He makes high quality traditional-style baskets, such as lidded rice or food containers, as well as producing a line of products, such as small camote trays, specifically designed to meet new consumer tastes. By alternating between these two types of production, Pedro has been able to increase his earnings and expand the time he spends in craft production. Indeed, Pedro has made two trips personally to Baguio City to sell his baskets to craft shop owners in the city's main tourist markets. He simply packs his baskets, such as large camote trays, in the

FIGURE 3.4
Large camote, or sweet potato, trays fill the luggage compartment of the bus that travels between Banaue and Baguio City, the administrative center of the Luzon highlands. The trays are destined for the tourist markets of Baguio City. The informality of the transportation system enables artisans to personally take their products to urban markets. Banaue, 1995.

luggage compartment of one of the two daily buses that travel between Banaue and Baguio City (fig. 3.4). As his family does not own rice fields, Pedro's participation in cultivation consists primarily of his wage work during harvest time. He is paid either in cash or in rice (which he prefers) to carry the bundles of rice that women have harvested from the fields to the home of the landowner. Through his individual initiatives in basket production and trade, Pedro has increased the income of his household and more firmly secured its position within the community.

USING BASKETS IN SACRED AND SECULAR SPHERES

In Banaue, baskets play important roles in ritual celebrations. They also participate in the secular sphere as functional domestic objects and as commodities available for sale to tourists. In each instance, the baskets used are the same material objects, but their meanings change depending upon the intent of the user and the context of their application. This section charts the life histories of some of Banaue's baskets by demonstrating the fluidity with which they move in and out of different situations and the accompanying shifts in their meanings.

Although missionary efforts in the early 1900s and especially since the Second World War have succeeded in converting the majority of Cordillera people to Christianity, the Ifugao actively maintain their animist traditions. During my time in Banaue, I had numerous opportunities to attend local Ifugao rituals, or *baki*, that attest to the vitality of ongoing indigenous beliefs.[6] My respondents confirm that they continue to believe that all matter has a life and meaning both in this world and in the next. The complex Ifugao cosmology includes an extensive pantheon of spirits, good and evil, who are assumed to be involved to varying degrees in the affairs of human beings (Barton 1946; 1955; Conklin 1980, 12–13). As a means of propitiating *anito* (spirits), community feasts are held in which animals are sacrificed and upland rice and woven textiles placed in locally made baskets are offered. The spirits of the ancestors consume the soul of the animal and the objects offered, leaving the meat and the clothes for the participants of the ceremony (see also Scott 1974, 192–93).

Sponsoring such feasts and redistributing part of their wealth through gifts of rice, meat, and traditional objects continue to be major avenues through which influential individuals and families maintain and validate their status in Ifugao society. In addition ritual performances are undertaken by all Ifugao to demonstrate their respect for their ancestors at particular rites of passage. These provide an ongoing stimulus for the production of local upland rice and for the production of traditional crafts such as baskets.

Ifugao ritual performances mark the stages in the life cycle: birth, marriage, illness, death. Certain baskets are indispensable components of each of these events. They provide visual statements that help sustain the still vibrant values and beliefs of the Ifugao. Sherry Ortner notes that ritual is a system of meanings conveyed by and for actors through the manipulation of symbolic objects and arrangements (1978, 4–5). As such, the aim of ritual is to achieve a "transformation of the participants, either of individuals into new statuses or a group into a new or renewed sense of community" (Russell and Cunningham 1989, 3). The use of ritual objects such as baskets manifests this transformation, materially documenting and marking these changes. Baskets in this context emerge as "key elaborating symbols . . . vehicles for sorting out complex and undifferentiated feelings and ideas, making them comprehensible [and] communicable to others" (Ortner 1973, 1340). The baskets used in Banaue rituals continue to chart the course of indigenous ceremony in a region that has undergone profound economic and cultural changes. The following account focuses on the use of baskets in mortuary and curing rites. My attendance at these ceremonies offered me the best opportunities to observe the performance of baskets in ritual contexts.

At all ceremonies, including births and marriages, large quantities of rice are cooked for the participants. The rice is often prepared earlier in the day, placed in rice baskets, and covered with banana leaves to protect it from insects and dirt (fig. 3.5). The public distribution of rice establishes the status of the host and ensures the community's good wishes for the celebrants of the ritual. Guests often comment on the amount of rice provided at the ritual in terms of the number of baskets used. Thus the baskets act as a symbolic measure of the host's generosity and as a material measure of the amount of rice served (fig. 3.6).

As containers of the life force, baskets play a particular role in the ceremonies that accompany death. In Banaue's extensive mortuary rites, the living descendants distribute part of their acquired wealth to the deceased so that the souls of their material belongings may escort the departed family member to the land of the dead. Relatives supply the deceased with all that he or she will need for a safe journey to the next world. In a rice winnowing basket, which functions as a symbol of fertility, relatives place a coconut shell filled with water along with ample rice, rice beer, cash, and betel and tobacco for chewing. Respondents explain, "We want to provide for our ancestors; we do not

FIGURE 3.5
Cooked rice fills food baskets covered with banana leaves. This food has been prepared for the participants at a marriage ceremony. The great number of baskets attests to the wealth and status of the host. Banaue, 1995.

FIGURE 3.6
Rice is customarily cooked in a wok over a wood fire and placed in a food basket for serving. Here a large amount of rice is prepared for a ritual celebration. Banaue, 1995.

want them to return to us asking for additional goods and causing misfortune and illness. Let this basket and the items we place in this container fulfill our relative's needs" (figs. 3.7, 3.8).

Baskets are similarly used in rites performed to cure a family member who is ill. In such rites, the appropriate food, objects, and clothing are offered to the ancestors whom the Ifugao believe have caused the illness due to their displeasure with the behavior of the living. These offerings are placed in or on top of a food container (fig. 3.9). The souls of the ancestors are formally invited to join the living where they actively participate in the ceremony and solicit offerings from their descendants in return for bestowing wealth and prosperity. This transformation is made visible by placing traditional, striped Ifugao textiles in a food basket and enticing the spirits to again clothe themselves in the garments (fig. 3.10). Again, the basket functions symbolically as

FIGURE 3.7
At mortuary rites, bundles of harvested rice, rice beer, water, and betel and tobacco for chewing are placed in a basket for the deceased. Chinese porcelain rice beer jars at the side of the basket attest to the wealth of this family. Banaue, 1995.

FIGURE 3.8 (ABOVE)
In this basket the family of the deceased have provided their relative with items required for a safe journey to the next world. These include cooked rice, betel leaves, meat, and coconut shells, which will be filled with beer and water. Banaue, 1995.

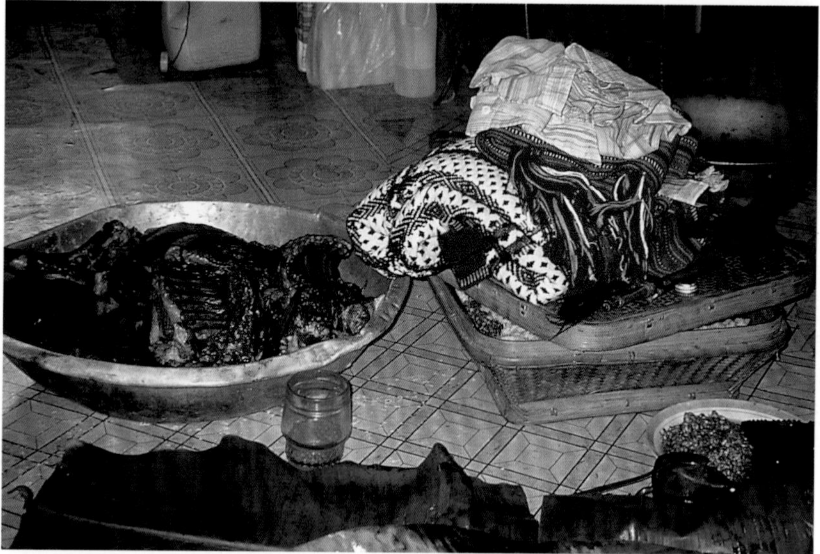

FIGURE 3.9 (BOTTOM RIGHT)
In curing rituals, the ancestors are placated through the appropriate offerings of food, such as meat and rice and clothing. These items are most often placed in or on top of a plaited food container. Banaue, 1995.

a container for the life force of the ancestors who are summoned during the ritual.

In both curing and mortuary rites, these baskets provide the focus for activities as the priest leading the ceremony directs all prayers to the container and its contents. Similar general rites may be performed at any time that the living want to appease and show their respect to their ancestors, either to acknowledge their good fortune or to dispel misfortune. The Ifugao believe that as soon as the living take the first steps toward satisfying their ancestors' desires through these offerings, the spirits will stop causing trouble (see also Ellis 1981, 227). Following the ceremony, each family personally decides whether or not to reintroduce the basket into domestic use.

Many of the baskets that perform in the ritual sphere are identical to those used for functional, everyday tasks. As one walks among Banaue house-

FIGURE 3.10
During curing rituals the clothes of the deceased are placed in a food basket, and the spirits of the family's ancestors are invited to join the living by again wearing their garments. Banaue, 1995.

holds scattered throughout the rice fields, for example, one inevitably hears the rhythmic sound of rice being pounded and the subsequent tossing of the rice in the winnowing basket as the hulls are separated from the rice kernels. Since a family of six to eight members might pound one bundle of rice (one kilo) per meal, the winnowing basket is constantly in use (fig. 3.11). Baskets are also used as containers to hold the family's communal meal of cooked food (rice, meat, and sweet potatoes; fig. 3.12). Indeed, the purchase of such a basket is conducted with great care. Local residents shopping for food containers examine the baskets offered for sale in Banaue town shops carefully judging the quality of the workmanship before making their choices.

In Ifugao baskets fulfill a number of other functional uses. Open-plaited baskets, for example, serve as containers in which to protect and keep chickens at night. Most traditional Ifugao houses located in the rice fields proudly display a row of these baskets hanging under the eaves to proclaim the family's

FIGURE 3.11
A teenage boy transfers pounded rice from the stone mortar to the winnowing tray in preparation for separating the rice kernels from the hulls. Banaue, 1995.

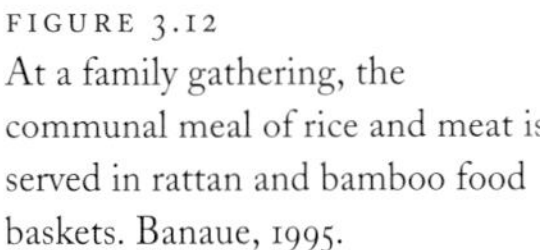

FIGURE 3.12
At a family gathering, the communal meal of rice and meat is served in rattan and bamboo food baskets. Banaue, 1995.

FIGURE 3.13
Baskets used for housing chickens hang from the eaves of a traditional Ifugao house. Banaue, 1995.

FIGURE 3.14 (MIDDLE LEFT)
Open-plaited baskets are used to contain a household's chickens and are hung from the eaves of the house. Banaue, 1995.

FIGURE 3.15 (MIDDLE RIGHT)
Open-plaited baskets used to hold a family's possessions are stored in the rafters under the house where the family can watch over them. Valuable possessions wrapped in traditional striped textiles are similarly stored under the house. Banaue, 1995.

FIGURE 3.16
A basket maker constructs an innovative type of chicken coop from plaited rattan, bamboo, and wood. Banaue, 1995.

FIGURE 3.17
A woman wears a plaited rattan and bamboo backpack to carry her personal possessions. Banaue, 1995.

wealth in livestock (figs. 3.13, 3.14). Indeed, similarly constructed round baskets are often seen under the eaves of the house where they are used to store both valuables and household possessions (fig. 3.15). In one of my visits to an artisan's home, I was able to observe the construction of a state-of-the-art chicken coop. The artisan, a basket maker, plaited lengths of rattan into a large rectangular 4' x 8' sheet and then bent this piece into an arch shape over a wooden base to fabricate this shelter for his chickens (fig. 3.16). Plaited rattan backpacks provide yet another example of traditional-style baskets that continue their life histories in contemporary circumstances. Previously used primarily by men to carry personal possessions and hunting implements, these baskets are now also increasingly used by young boys to carry their school supplies and by women to carry a variety of small items they need to transport (fig. 3.17).

Understanding the significance of contemporary Ifugao baskets means considering the different phases of their biographies and how their meanings shift according to the contexts within which they function. The production of traditional Ifugao baskets such as winnowing trays and rice containers, for example (cat. nos. 2, 8), is thus stimulated by their integral roles in Banaue's ongoing ritual activities as well as by their continual need as everyday, functional objects. Added to these spheres of production, moreover, is the demand for new types of baskets designed for tourists' tastes.

INNOVATION IN TRADITIONAL BASKETMAKING PRACTICES

Since the mid-1980s, the efforts of the federal government's Department of Trade and Industry to promote the export of Philippine handicrafts has resulted in an increased demand for wooden, coconut-shell, and bamboo containers decorated with rattan basketry. Women are the primary artisans in this new craft form. Building on the region's tradition of producing coiled baskets, such as the rice containers illustrated in catalog numbers 4 and 5, women have adapted this technique to develop a range of new basket products. Weavers especially may transform their skills in cloth production to those required for basketmaking. Depending upon the demand, they may work either full or part-time, often alternating between these two crafts. In so doing, they have improved their earnings and their personal status within the community. Those artisans who have accumulated some capital buy the wood forms from local carvers and the coconut shells and rattan from lowland vendors; others secure their basket materials and wooden forms from the trader commissioning the order and work on a piecework basis. Neither craft, weaving nor basketry, is more prestigious than the other, but the growing tourist market for baskets means that this craft can provide a more continuous and dependable source of income for artisans.

The women engaged in basketmaking use the same materials as men but tend to focus on different types of products and on different techniques. In basketmaking, women use an overcast, or coiling, technique to wrap rattan around a central core that is then attached to the edges of wooden forms and coconut shells as a decorative finish. In Banaue, artisans refer to this technique as "knitting," or the *tari* technique. Artisans also knot or twist the rattan in

FIGURE 3.18
Women decorate bamboo forms and coconut shells with plaited rattan. These new products have been developed by female artisans particularly to meet the demands of new consumer tastes. They are sold in the local and regional tourist markets in Banaue and Baguio City. Banaue, 1995.

FIGURE 3.19
This basket maker is finishing a plaited basket by coiling rattan on the upper third of the piece. Banaue, 1995.

various lacework arrangements to cover the outer surface of bamboo and coconut-shell forms and containers (fig. 3.18). Only a few women use the plaiting technique employed by men to construct baskets (fig. 3.19). Some men, however, are now learning how to embellish wooden containers in the *tari* technique and often work with women in applying this decorative rattan finish (see fig. 3.18).

Artisans working with their own materials prefer to fill specific orders from craft traders. Failing this, they produce the most popular items and either take them to Banaue's craft shops or give them, on consignment, to other traders selling in larger urban centers such as Manila or Baguio City. Some of the products artisans commonly make include a variety of animal-shaped containers, circular trays, and wooden bowls and bamboo forms decorated with rattan in various basketmaking techniques. Indeed, this opportunity for many female artisans in particular to develop new products means that some women have been able to make the leap from producer to producer-trader status.

Ruth Matagan, for example, thirty-two and a widow with four children, supports her family with her basketmaking business. When her husband died in 1993, she used her savings from her basket piecework to start her own business. Ruth works hard to develop a patron-client, or *suki*, relationship with four buyers to ensure that she obtains continuous orders. She purchases her own rattan and bamboo from lowland vendors and negotiates with local carvers to buy their wooden bowls at the best price. Ruth tries to obtain commissions for decorated bowls and trays, rather than containers, as she can complete the former in less time and thus realize a better profit. With a small rice field that provides her family with six months of rice, Ruth has been able to continue her business without accruing debts. Through her basket production and trade, she has improved her personal position and that of her family.

CONCLUSION

Banaue artisans continue to produce both traditional- and commercial-style baskets. In so doing, they demonstrate the cultural and economic importance of basketmaking to rural households and establish baskets as a medium of communication that operates within and among communities. Baskets are used as functional objects in daily, domestic tasks; they perform as ritual objects; and they serve as mementos for tourists. As such baskets develop their own personal "biographies"; they embody different meanings for the different people who make, use, buy, and recontextualize them (Kopytoff 1986, 66–67).

FIGURE 3.20
Shop selling baskets. Banaue, 1998.

To the artisans, for example, baskets represent the makers' knowledge and skills and their ability to accumulate the economic resources necessary for the object's manufacture. Income from basketmaking enables artisan families to meet their subsistence needs and to secure a respected position within the community. Local Banaue consumers take pride in the number and quality of baskets that their households use in everyday tasks and display in rituals; the number of baskets owned by a family demonstrates its consumer power. To travelers visiting Ifugao, baskets emerge as a metaphor for and a memento of a unique and exotic place (Gordon 1986). Dominguez argues that what we collect tells us something about ourselves (1986, 554). Thus, travelers displaying their purchase of baskets at home may feel that this object indicates their interest in other peoples and cultures, their travel initiative, their connoisseurship, and their identity as collectors (Clifford 1988, 220). To the Banaue craft trader conducting the sale between the artisan and the consumer, the meaning of the object centers on its economic exchange value.[7] Thus a number of "contextual referents are collapsed into a single . . . object or visual marker" (Jules-Rosette 1986, 56).

Banaue basket makers straddle a difficult line: on the one side, they strive to maintain the sphere of traditional production and their personal artistic preferences; on the other side, they try to be responsive to the exigencies of consumer tastes (figs. 3.20, 3.21). This case study demonstrates that artisans have been largely successful in juggling these two positions. Indeed, their versatility has been a strong underpinning of the continuing vitality of baskets through multiple transformations. By pursuing traditional basketmaking practices while embracing the new markets that have developed in the late twentieth century, many Banaue basket makers have been able to enhance their personal positions and those of their households. Thus, the multidimensional circumstances of contemporary basketmaking in Banaue not only produce and market desirable commodities but also reproduce and market Ifugao ethnic identity and social institutions.[8]

FIGURE 3.21
As commonly seen, this woman is using both rattan and mass-produced plastic baskets. Banaue, 1998.

CHAPTER 4

Catalog of the Exhibition

Roy W. Hamilton

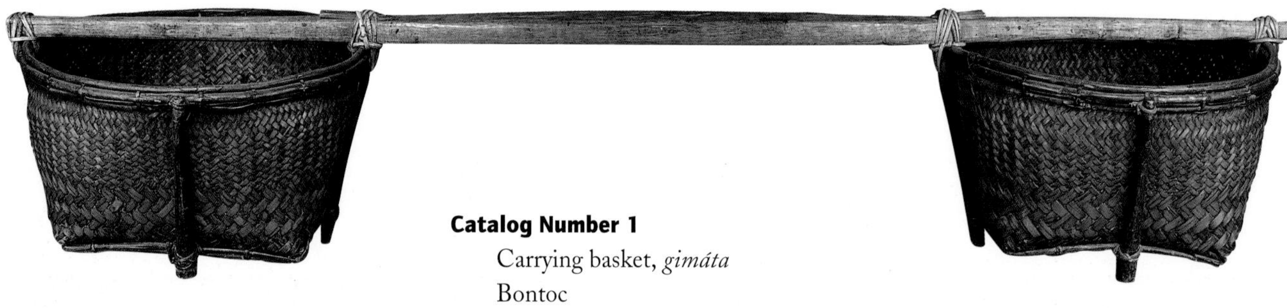

Catalog Number 1

Carrying basket, *gimáta*
Bontoc
Plaited construction
Bamboo
Length 172 cm
FMCH X78.2305; Gift of Helen and Dr. Robert Kuhn

Bontoc men attach a *gimáta*, or carrying basket, to each end of a pole that is then placed across the shoulders. These baskets are typically used for carrying sweet potatoes or newly harvested rice; although they come in handy for transporting other things as well, including manure, which the Bontoc carry to their fields from the stone-lined pits where they raise pigs.

Cat. no. 1, detail

FIGURE 4.1
These Bontoc men use carrying baskets (*gimáta*), attached to each end of a pole, to convey newly harvested rice back to the village. Women share in this task, but they typically carry single baskets on their heads. Early twentieth century. Day Collection, Fowler Museum of Cultural History.

Catalog Number 2

Winnowing tray, *liga-u*
Ifugao
Plaited construction
Rattan
Width 69 cm
FMCH X78.2382; Gift of Helen and Dr. Robert Kuhn

FIGURE 4.2
An Ifugao youth winnows rice. The deep square tray laid on the ground to catch the chaff is a true Ifugao *liga-u*. The flat tray he holds in his hand, however, is not a local style and was purchased from the Kalinga region. The chaff, which also contains broken grains, will be fed to the family's poultry. Banaue, 1997.

The traditional winnowing tray of the Ifugao is a square basket made of rattan. Rice is winnowed in the tray after it has been hulled, a process that involves pounding it in a mortar with a heavy loglike pestle. When the tray is used for winnowing, the lashed join on its rim is oriented away from the winnower; this keeps the heavy weight of the grain, which is held close to the winnower's body, away from the weakest point of the rim.

In addition to its function as a winnowing tray, this basket is sometimes also used for communal eating. In this case, cooked rice is placed around the outer part of the basket with a bowl of meat or soup in the center.

Catalog Number 3

Winnowing tray, *lig-o*
Bontoc
Plaited construction
Bamboo, rattan
Width 70 cm
FMCH X86.3392; Gift of Helen and Dr. Robert Kuhn

The round shape of the Bontoc winnowing tray serves to distinguish it from the square Ifugao tray (cat. no. 2). According to Jenks (1905, 125), the Bontoc trays are made primarily in the villages of Samoki and Kanyu.

FIGURE 4.3
A Bontoc girl winnows rice using the round Bontoc winnowing tray (*lig-o*). She has removed the pounded grain from the double-chambered mortar in front of her. Early twentieth century. Day Collection, Fowler Museum of Cultural History.

Catalog Number 4

Jar-shaped rice storage basket,
ulbung
Ifugao
Coiled construction
Rattan
Height 19 cm
FMCH X86.3390a,b; Gift of Helen
and Dr. Robert Kuhn

The jar-shaped *ulbung* is one of the most distinctive Ifugao baskets. It was formerly found in all Ifugao households, where it was used to store hulled rice, and is one of the few types of baskets in the Cordillera constructed using the coiling technique. Its graceful curved form is modeled after ceramic jars of Chinese origin that have long been highly prized in the Cordillera as storage containers for rice beer and as heirlooms. This example is of particularly fine construction, but its handle is missing.

FIGURE 4.4
Imported Chinese ceramic jars, which the Ifugao use for storing rice beer, serve as the model for the shape of the *ulbung*. The jars, decorated in a variety of styles and colors, are highly prized by the Ifugao, and each type has a clearly defined value. Fowler Museum of Cultural History X97.40.1; Gift of Jovita Luglug.

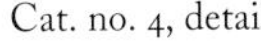

Cat. no. 4, detail

FIGURE 4.5
A basket maker in Tam-an village, Banaue, completes the lid for a newly made *ulbung*. Banaue basket makers currently use rattan purchased from the nearby lowlands. 1997.

Catalog Number 5

Jar-shaped rice storage basket,
ulbung
Ifugao
Coiled construction
Rattan
Height 27 cm
FMCH X78.2329a,b; Gift of Helen
and Dr. Robert Kuhn

The *ulbung* may be hung by its handle to keep it safe from rats or other pests. Even a large *ulbung* such as this one will hold only enough rice to provide for the needs of the family for one or two days. In most Ifugao households a fresh supply of rice is milled every day.

Catalog Number 6

Basket for storing husked rice, *kamuwan*
Bontoc
Plaited construction
Bamboo, rattan, wood
Height 34 cm
FMCH X78.2242a,b; Gift of Helen and Dr. Robert Kuhn

The *kamuwan* is used for storing milled rice or legumes in the house. It is the Bontoc equivalent of the Ifugao *ulbung* (cat. nos. 4, 5) and shares a similar jarlike shape.

Catalog Number 7

Basket, *kamuwan*
Kankanay
Plaited construction
Bamboo, rattan
Height 35 cm
FMCH X82.1221a,b; Museum purchase with Manus Fund

This Kankanay *kamuwan* has lizard-shaped handles, a decorative touch that has been widely copied in recent years by basket makers in the commercial trade. A *kamuwan* of this size holds more rice than is needed for daily requirements and would probably have been used in preparation for a celebration involving many guests.

FIGURE 4.6
A *hū'up* filled with rice and cooked chicken forms part of a ritual offering at a *honga* ceremony in Banaue, 1997. The *honga* is held to secure improved health for an ailing relative. Concealed among the offerings is a tape recorder, which the sponsor of the ceremony used to record the chanting of the ritual leaders.

Catalog Number 8

Food basket, *hū'up*
Ifugao
Plaited construction
Bamboo, rattan
Width 42 cm
FMCH X78.2335a,b; Gift of Helen and Dr. Robert Kuhn

The square, lidded *hū'up* is another characteristic Ifugao basket; it is used for serving cooked rice in the household. It is designed for communal eating and holds rice for the entire group assembled for the meal. The *hū'up* can also be used to carry food to workers in the rice fields. This is in contrast to the Bontoc practice of using individual lunch boxes (cat. nos. 10, 12). Additionally, the *hū'up* appears at special ceremonial events, where it is used to hold cooked rice and meat.

The *hū'up* has a special role in the engagement process of an Ifugao couple. The family of the prospective groom acquires a *hū'up* and fills it with betel leaves, areca nuts, cooked rice, and cooked chicken. These goods are presented to the family of the prospective bride at the engagement ceremony. Today cash may be included as well. Afterward, the container becomes the property of the new couple and is used in their household for the serving of cooked rice.

Catalog Number 9

Basket for cooked rice, *ákob*
Bontoc
Plaited construction
Bamboo, rattan, wood
Width 35 cm
FMCH X78.2340a,b; Gift of Helen and Dr. Robert Kuhn

The round Bontoc *ákob* is the equivalent of the square Ifugao *hū'up* (cat. no. 8) and is used primarily to serve cooked rice. When shown this basket, a Bontoc visitor to the Fowler Museum commented that not everyone would be able to afford such a luxurious basket and only particularly skilled basket makers would be able to make one.

Cat. no. 9, detail

Catalog Number 10

Lunch box, *tópil*
Bontoc
Plaited construction
Bamboo, rattan
Height 11 cm
FMCH X78.2306a,b; Gift of Helen and Dr. Robert Kuhn

The *tópil* is the Bontoc "lunch box"; it is used by individual workers to carry food to the fields to sustain themselves through a long day of work. *Tópil* of differing forms are made in the various Bontoc villages. This square-shaped *tópil* is considered to be the typical style of the central Bontoc region, including Bontoc town and the surrounding area. It would once have had a cordlike handle threaded through the loops on the lid to keep the lid attached and to provide for ease in carrying.

Catalog Number 11

Basket for cooked rice, *tópil*
Bontoc
Plaited construction
Bamboo, rattan, wood, wire
Height 18 cm
FMCH X78.2254a,b; Gift of Helen and Dr. Robert Kuhn

Unusually large *tópil*, like this one, are sometimes used to carry cooked rice and meat to celebrations such as weddings. At a Bontoc wedding, the in-laws cannot eat together until they have exchanged the meat and rice that they have each brought to the celebration in such containers.

Opposite: cat. no. 11, detail

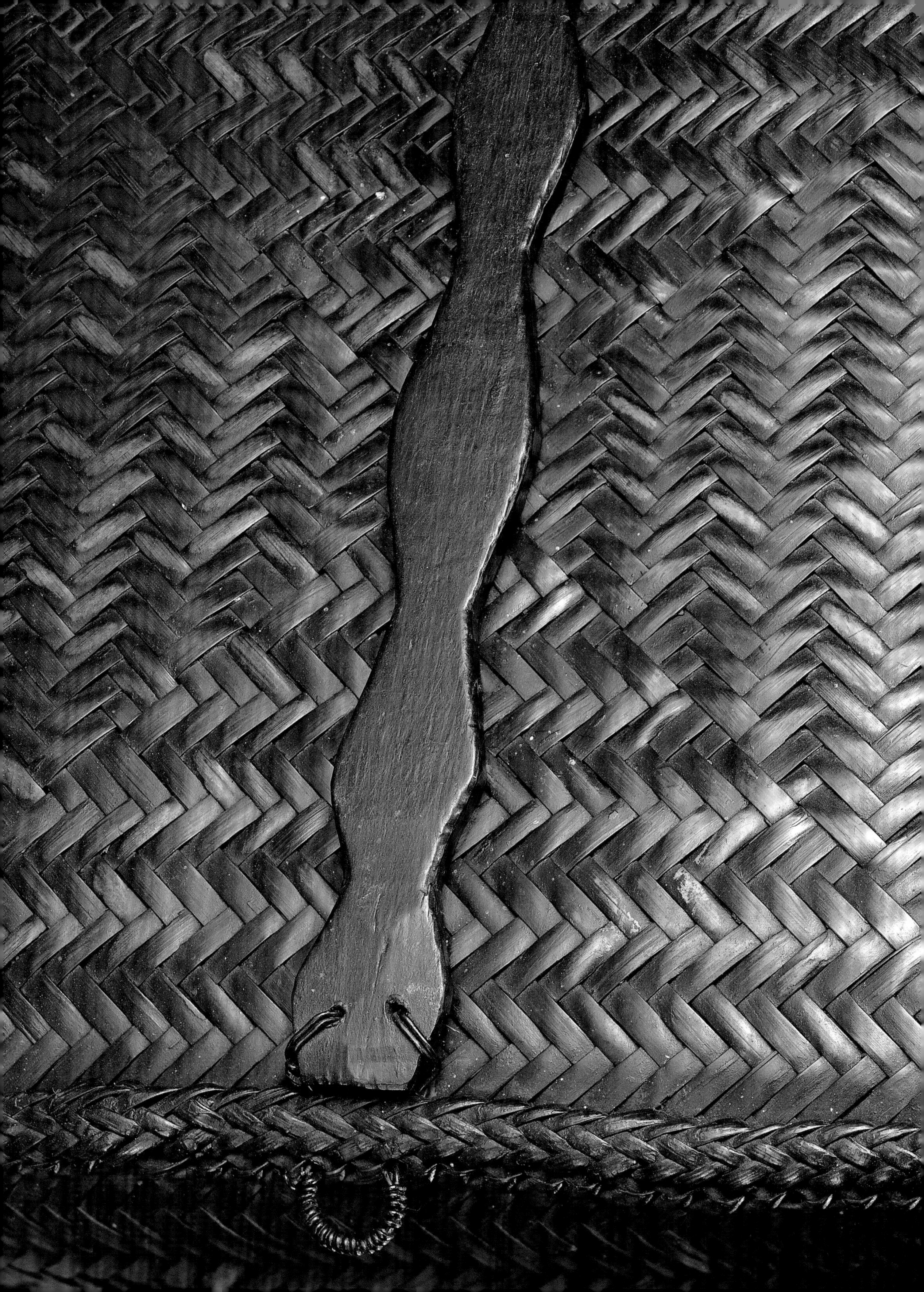

Catalog Number 12

Basket for cooked rice, *ákob*
Bontoc
Plaited construction
Bamboo, wood, rattan
Width 23 cm
FMCH X76.212a,b; Museum purchase with Manus Fund

This basket is probably from the region of Sagada Village rather than central Bontoc. It was presumably used to carry food to the fields, just as the central Bontoc *tópil* is (cat. no. 10).

Cat. no. 13, bottom

Catalog Number 13

Plate, *giyag*
Bontoc
Plaited construction
Bamboo, rattan
Length 22 cm
FMCH X78.2270; Gift of Helen and Dr. Robert Kuhn

The *giyag* is an individual serving plate used for ceremonial occasions. Jenks (1905, 123) reported that *giyag* were made in all the Bontoc villages, but he had difficulty purchasing them due to their ceremonial associations. The Ifugao do not have a corresponding plate for individual servings, but they sometimes employ a small *hū'up* for this purpose.

Catalog Number 14

Basket for roasted unripe rice, *kulikug*
Bontoc
Plaited construction
Bamboo, rattan
Height 20 cm
FMCH X78.2265; Gift of Helen and Dr. Robert Kuhn

This unusually shaped basket is designed to store *chu-um*, or roasted green rice, which the Bontoc relish as a snack. The rice grains are harvested while soft, before they are fully ripened. They are then roasted and pounded in the rice mortar to remove the hull. This flattens the soft grains, which are eaten without further cooking. The closed form of the basket helps keep the grains soft, as they quickly harden with exposure to the air.

Catalog Number 15

Jar for rice beer, *hinoghogan*
Ifugao
Plaited construction
Clay, rattan, wood
Height 16 cm
FMCH X76.1065a,b

The *hinoghogan* is a ceramic jar with a protective covering made of rattan. Although it could be used to hold a variety of substances, its most exalted function is as a container for rice beer to be used as an offering at a ceremony. The containers are rare in the Ifugao regions and are mostly owned by priests, who use them in conducting rites. Because of their rarity, *hinoghogan* are often borrowed when required for a ceremony.

Catalog Number 16

Sieve for rice beer, *gūbun di bayah*
Ifugao
Plaited construction
Bamboo
Length 44 cm
FMCH X78.2180; Gift of Helen and Dr. Robert Kuhn

A *gūbu* is a tapering, tubular trap for fish (cat. nos. 38, 39). The *gūbun di bayah* (a sieve for rice beer, or *bayah*) is very similar in shape. The Ifugao store rice beer, together with its fermented rice mash, in ceramic jars of Chinese origin. To separate the beer from the mash, the *gūbun di bayah* is pushed down into the center of the jar. The liquid flows into the sieve, while the mash is kept outside. A bamboo dipper is then used to extract the beer from the center of the sieve.

FIGURE 4.7
A *gūbun di bayah* sits inside a jar of rice beer. Banaue, 1997.

Catalog Number 17

Carrying basket for sweet potatoes, *kayabang*
Ibaloi
Plaited construction
Rattan, wood
Height 47 cm
FMCH X78.2320a,b; Gift of Helen and Dr. Robert Kuhn

Among the Ibaloi people of Benguet Province, women use a *kayabang*, a basket with a round rim that tapers to a square base, to transport sweet potatoes and other root crops, such as yams, cassava, or taro. The basket is carried by means of a strap worn across the forehead.

FIGURE 4.8
An Ibaloi woman carries taro leaves home in a *kayabang*. Early twentieth century. Day Collection, Fowler Museum of Cultural History.

Catalog Number 18

Carrying basket for sweet potatoes, *balyag*
Ifugao
Plaited construction
Rattan
Height 71 cm
FMCH X78.2245; Gift of Helen and Dr. Robert Kuhn

The Ifugao sweet potato basket, or *balyag*, is distinguished from the *kayabang* of the Ibaloi people of Benguet Province (cat. no. 17) by its square profile. This *balyag* would have originally had a forehead strap, but straps are often removed when baskets enter the commercial art trade. Like the Ibaloi *kayabang*, the Ifugao *balyag* is carried exclusively by women.

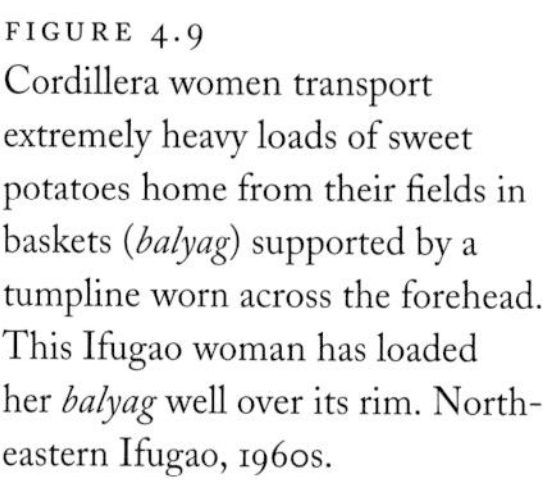

FIGURE 4.9
Cordillera women transport extremely heavy loads of sweet potatoes home from their fields in baskets (*balyag*) supported by a tumpline worn across the forehead. This Ifugao woman has loaded her *balyag* well over its rim. Northeastern Ifugao, 1960s.

Opposite: cat. no. 18, detail

Catalog Number 19

Carrying basket for sweet potatoes, *allataw*
Ifugao
Plaited construction
Rattan
Height 46 cm
FMCH X78.2240; Gift of Helen and Dr. Robert Kuhn

The *allataw* is a shorter version of the *balyag* (cat. no. 18) and is also used to transport root crops. Both types of baskets are considered specialty products of the Ifugao village of Cambulo.

Catalog Number 20

Basket for vegetables, *awit*
Kalinga
Plaited construction
Rattan, bamboo
Height 29 cm
FMCH X78.2233; Gift of Helen and
Dr. Robert Kuhn

Kalinga women use a heavy, round basket (*awit*) for carrying bundles of newly harvested rice, root crops, or vegetables. Unlike the Ibaloi and Ifugao baskets with forehead straps (cat. nos. 17, 18), the strapless *awit* is carried on top of the head. The thick braided hoop of heavy rattan encircling the basket provides added strength to its structure.

Catalog Number 21

Basket for vegetables, *labba*
Tinguian
Plaited construction
Bamboo
Width 37 cm
FMCH X78.2228; Gift of Helen and Dr. Robert Kuhn

Tinguian women carry their burden baskets on their heads, like their Kalinga counterparts (cat. no. 20). This basket is of much lighter construction than the Kalinga *awit*, however, and appears to be based on an Ilocano style of basketry. Many aspects of Tinguian material culture show evidence of a degree of assimilation with lowland Ilocano neighbors.

FIGURE 4.10
This Tinguian mother manages to keep her hands free by carrying her child on her back and her basket on her head. Reproduced from Worcester (1912, 923).

Catalog Number 22

Basket for storing raw cotton,
kolang
Tinguian
Plaited construction
Bamboo, rattan, wood
Length 71 cm
FMCH X78.2260; Gift of Helen and Dr. Robert Kuhn

This huge basket (*kolang*) with a carrying handle was used by the Tinguian people of Abra Province during the cotton harvest. The hot dry climate and lower elevation of Abra made it a productive cotton-growing region.

Catalog Number 23

Hunter's backpack, *inabnūtan*
Ifugao
Plaited construction
Rattan, *abnut* fiber from the *bangi* palm
Height 56 cm
FMCH X82.1524; Promised gift of the Rogers Family Foundation

The *inabnūtan* takes its name from a fiber called *abnut*, which is processed from the leaf stalk of the *bangi* palm. The basket is covered with this fiber in order to repel the rain. Baskets of this type were formerly used by Ifugao men when journeying far from their home village. On the outbound journey, the pack held the hunter's provisions, including perhaps a jar of rice beer with which to make offerings to insure a successful hunt. If luck and skill prevailed, the men returned to the village with their packs filled with meat.

FIGURE 4.11
This early twentieth-century photograph shows a gathering of Ifugao men and boys, several of whom wear the traditional backpack (*inabnūtan*). Courtesy of Peabody Museum of Archaeology and Ethnology, Harvard University.

Cat. no. 23, back

Catalog Number 24

Backpack, *fangao*
Bontoc
Plaited construction
Bamboo, rattan, palm fiber
Height 47 cm
FMCH X86.3374; Gift of Helen and
Dr. Robert Kuhn

The Bontoc *fangao* is used to carry provisions when traveling away from home, as is the Ifugao *inabnūtan* (cat. no. 23). These baskets have sometimes been called "head baskets" in reference to the former Cordillera practice of head-hunting, but the term is misleading as the baskets were really used to transport any kind of supply. According to Jenks (1905, 122), *fangao* were made in the villages of Ambawan, Barlig, and Kanyu.

FIGURE 4.12
The everyday utility of basketry items is evident in both the hat and backpack shown in this photo of an Ifugao man walking to his rice terraces. The style of backpack he uses is common to both the Bontoc, who call it *sangi*, and the Ifugao, who call it *hapē'eng*. Near Banaue, 1969.

Catalog Number 25

Backpack, *hapē'eng*
Ifugao
Plaited construction
Rattan
Height 38 cm
FMCH X78.2276a,b; Gift of Helen and Dr. Robert Kuhn

Hapē'eng is the name the Ifugao use for their everyday backpacks, which are made in a variety of regional styles. This type of *hapē'eng*, which is identified by its heavy rattan hoops, comes from the Ifugao town of Mayaoyao. The hoops provide a rigid structure that enables the backpack to be used as a stool by a weary traveler.

Overleaf: cat. no. 25, detail

Catalog Number 26

Backpack, *sangi*
Bontoc
Plaited construction
Rattan
Height 40 cm
FMCH X86.3364a,b; Gift of Helen and Dr. Robert Kuhn

The Bontoc *sangi* is an everyday backpack much like the Ifugao *hapē'eng* (cat. no. 25). This *sangi* features a heavy, plaited rattan shoulder strap.

Opposite: cat. no. 25, detail

Catalog Number 27

Container for meat, *lóden*
Bontoc
Coiled construction
Coconut shell, rattan, wood
Height 14 cm
x96.5.38a,b; Bequest of Alan Rose

This container made of a coconut shell was used to store meat. It is strengthened with a rattan netting, and its mouth is narrowed by additional rattan, which has been worked in the coiling technique and sealed with resin. Because of its small size, it was probably used to store only a single day's supply of fresh meat. The Bontoc, however, routinely preserved pork or water buffalo meat for up to three years in similar, but larger, containers made of gourds. This meat, called *ittag*, was preserved with salt.

Catalog Number 28

Storage basket, *tayaan*
Bontoc
Plaited construction
Bamboo, rattan, wood
Length 51 cm
FMCH x78.2318a,b; Gift of Helen and Dr. Robert Kuhn

The *tayaan* is a general-purpose storage basket, which could be used to hold a large quantity of hulled rice, clothing, or other household items. Due to its large size and fine workmanship, Bontoc informants on viewing this basket remarked that it had most likely been in the possession of a relatively well-to-do household.

Cat. no. 28

Cat. no. 28, detail

Catalog Number 29

Basket for storing spoons, *ayyud*
Ifugao
Plaited construction
Rattan
Height 21 cm
FMCH X78.2286; Gift of Helen and Dr. Robert Kuhn

While most Cordillera people routinely ate with their hands, the Ifugao were known for carving beautiful spoons. In many Ifugao households each person had an individual spoon. After eating, spoons were wiped and put away in an openwork basket (*ayyud*).

Catalog Number 30

Basket for carrying gongs, *balen di gangha*
Ifugao
Plaited construction
Rattan
Height 39 cm
FMCH X78.2287; Gift of Helen and Dr. Robert Kuhn

The term *balen* is derived from *bale*, or house. *Balen di gangha* means literally a "house for a gong," a basket used to transport the instrument wherever it is to be played. The gong is the most important instrument in Ifugao ceremonial contexts. The curvilinear decorative work added to this basket represents the predilections of an individual basket maker and is not found on all gong "houses."

FIGURE 4.13
Basketry chicken coops (*ubi*) hang from the floor beams of an Ifugao house. Early twentieth century. Day Collection, Fowler Museum of Cultural History.

Catalog Number 31

Chicken coop, *ubi*
Ifugao
Plaited construction
Rattan, wood
Height 49 cm
FMCH X91.5694; Gift of Mr. and Mrs. Louis Marienthal

Chickens, along with dogs and pigs, are the characteristic domestic animals of the Cordillera and throughout the Austronesian realm. Ifugao chickens run free during the day but are confined at night to keep them safe from predators and thieves. They are kept in special baskets (*ubi*) that hang well above ground, under the floor beam of the raised house.

FIGURE 4.14
The Bontoc used a basket very much like the Ifugao *alubī'ub*. When intercommunity warfare prevailed in the Bontoc region, trellislike ceremonial structures, or *komis*, were built along the trails connecting warring villages. Chickens and pigs were brought to the *komis* to be sacrificed and eaten by the warriors. Baskets for carrying chickens can be seen hanging on the posts at this Bontoc *komis*, and one of the posts consists of a tree-fern stem carved into a figure of an *anito*, or spirit. Reproduced from Jenks (1905, pl. cxxvii).

Catalog Number 32

Basket for carrying chickens,
alubī'ub
Ifugao
Plaited construction
Rattan
Length 33 cm
FMCH X78.2339; Gift of Helen and
Dr. Robert Kuhn

Today the *alubī'ub* is used for mundane purposes, such as taking a chicken to market. Ifugao elders, however, tend to equate this type of basket with more sacred endeavors because in the past, it was used to carry chickens to ritual sites in the mountains surrounding the villages. At such sites, the birds were sacrificed in various healing or warfare rituals. This basket was also used to carry a chicken to the forest where it would serve as a decoy to attract wild fowl.

Catalog Number 33

Sieve for catching snails, *haydu*
Ifugao
Plaited construction
Bamboo, rattan
Width 47 cm
FMCH X86.3393; Gift of Helen and
Dr. Robert Kuhn

The *haydu* is used chiefly by women as a sieve for capturing edible snails in the rice paddies. Snails are caught following the rice harvest when the stubble is cleaned out of the paddy fields. Ifugao rice terraces are kept filled with water all year, unlike the paddies in many rice-growing areas, which are allowed to dry out as the rice ripens.

This style of *haydu* is made in the northern sections of the Ifugao territory, including the villages of Cambulo and Mayaoyao. In the *haydu* of Banaue and the central Ifugao region, the slats of the sieve cross on the diagonal.

FIGURE 4.15
An Ifugao woman sifts through the mud in a flooded rice terrace to capture snails and other small aquatic animals. Near Banaue, 1960s.

FIGURE 4.16
Sievelike baskets similar to the *haydu* are used for a variety of tasks throughout the Cordillera. Here a Bontoc woman prepares sweet potato leaves, a popular vegetable in the Philippines. 1978.

Catalog Number 34

Basket for snails, *aggawin*
Bontoc
Plaited and twined construction
Bamboo, rattan, wood, plant fiber cord
Width 14 cm
FMCH X78.2249; Gift of Helen and Dr. Robert Kuhn

Cordillera rice fields are crisscrossed with snail tracks. When working in the fields, Bontoc women frequently carry the *aggawin* tied around their hips. When a woman finds an edible snail, which is considered a delicacy, she gathers it and puts it into the *aggawin* to carry home for the evening meal. The basket can also be used in gathering eggs or any other edibles encountered during the day's work.

Catalog Number 35

Locust storage basket, *iwus*
Bontoc
Twined construction
Bamboo, rattan
Height 58 cm
FMCH X86.3272

In the past, the Cordillera was at times beset by swarms of locusts, which were considered as much a delicacy as paddy snails. Jenks describes the manner in which these insects were captured by the Bontoc:

> The locusts come in storms, literally like a pelting, large-flaked snow-storm, driving across the country for hours or even days at a time. . . . The locust catcher runs along in the storm, and, whirling around in it with his large net, scoops in the victims. Many families sometimes wander a week or more catching locusts when they come to their vicinity, and cease only when miles from home. [1905, 143]

Once captured, the locusts could be kept alive in large, open-slatted storage baskets. They were prepared to eat by first boiling and then drying. This Bontoc locust basket, or *iwus*, is a particularly rare example; its decorations were carved into the freshly cut bamboo with a knife.

Cat. no. 35

FIGURE 4.17
These Ifugao women are roasting locusts over a fire. The basket behind them is apparently full of the insects, whose legs can be seen protruding through the slats. The Ifugao once made several different styles of locust baskets, all called *butit* (cat. no. 37), but the example in this photo is nearly identical to the Bontoc *iwus* (cat. no. 35) in the exhibition. Early twentieth century. Day Collection, Fowler Museum of Cultural History.

Catalog Number 36

Locust storage basket, *bocus*
Kalinga
Plaited construction
Rattan, bamboo
Height 47 cm
FMCH X78.2192a,b

Each Cordillera group had its own style of basket for storing locusts. The Kalinga version, called *bocus*, was a large jar-shaped basket with relatively tightly woven sides. The bottom of the basket has a grill-like netting that allows air to circulate inside. Originally, the basket would have had a lid, but this is now missing.

Catalog Number 37

Locust storage basket, *butit*
Ifugao
Twined construction
Bamboo, rattan
Height 42 cm
FMCH X78.2197; Gift of Helen and
Dr. Robert Kuhn

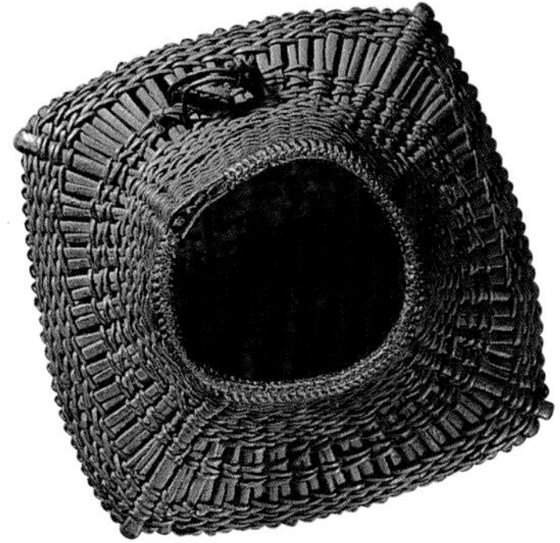

The Ifugao locust basket, or *butit*, has open-slatted sides constructed with the twining technique. Barton describes how the Ifugao prepared locusts as a food and stored them for future use: "They are first boiled; second, the wings and feet are pulled off; third, they are dried in the sun till perfectly dry and consequently very brittle; fourth, they are pounded into a powder and stored away in tightly-stoppered bamboo tubes" (1922, 395).

Catalog Number 38

Fish trap, *gūbu*
Ifugao
Plaited construction
Bamboo, rattan
Length 20 cm
FMCH x86.3356; Gift of Helen and
Dr. Robert Kuhn

Small fish traps (*gūbu*) of this type are set in the mud of the rice terraces to catch tiny fish. The trap is submerged in the mud, and the opening, which faces up, is smeared with a bit of fermented rice mash (left over from the making of rice beer) to attract the fish. It may also be sheltered from the sun with a bunch of leaves or grass, which help to form a shaded nook that is also attractive to the fish. Once a fish has passed through the funnel-shaped mouth of the trap, it is unable to get out again. *Gūbu* are normally used from the time just after harvest (around late September) until the next crop is partly grown (March). They are not set when the plants are more fully developed, however, as this might damage the crop.

Traps of this sort are often tended by children, who are given the task of setting them at dusk and collecting them in the morning. It is not unusual to set as many as fifty traps. During the day, the traps are carried back to the household, where they may often be seen hanging in bunches from house posts to dry in the sun.

Because large quantities of the traps are used, they are typically made rather quickly from readily available materials. The stem of the *bī'al* plant, a vine that grows in the steep, brush-covered slopes surrounding the rice terraces, is a material that is often used to make traps in the villages near Banaue.

FIGURE 4.18
Fish traps are hung to dry in the morning sun. These traps are not made from the usual basketry materials, rattan and bamboo, but from a vinelike plant called *bī'al*. Tam-an village, Banaue, 1997.

FIGURE 4.19
A young man collects the long flexible stems of the *bī'al* plant. Tam-an village, Banaue, 1997.

Catalog Number 39

Fish trap, *gūbu*
Ifugao
Twined construction
Palm midrib, rattan, plant fiber
Length 34 cm
x78.2261a; Gift of Helen and
Dr. Robert Kuhn

Large fish traps are set in the streams that water the Ifugao rice terraces. These traps are set with their conical mouths facing upstream so that fish will be carried into them by the current.

Cat. no. 39, detail

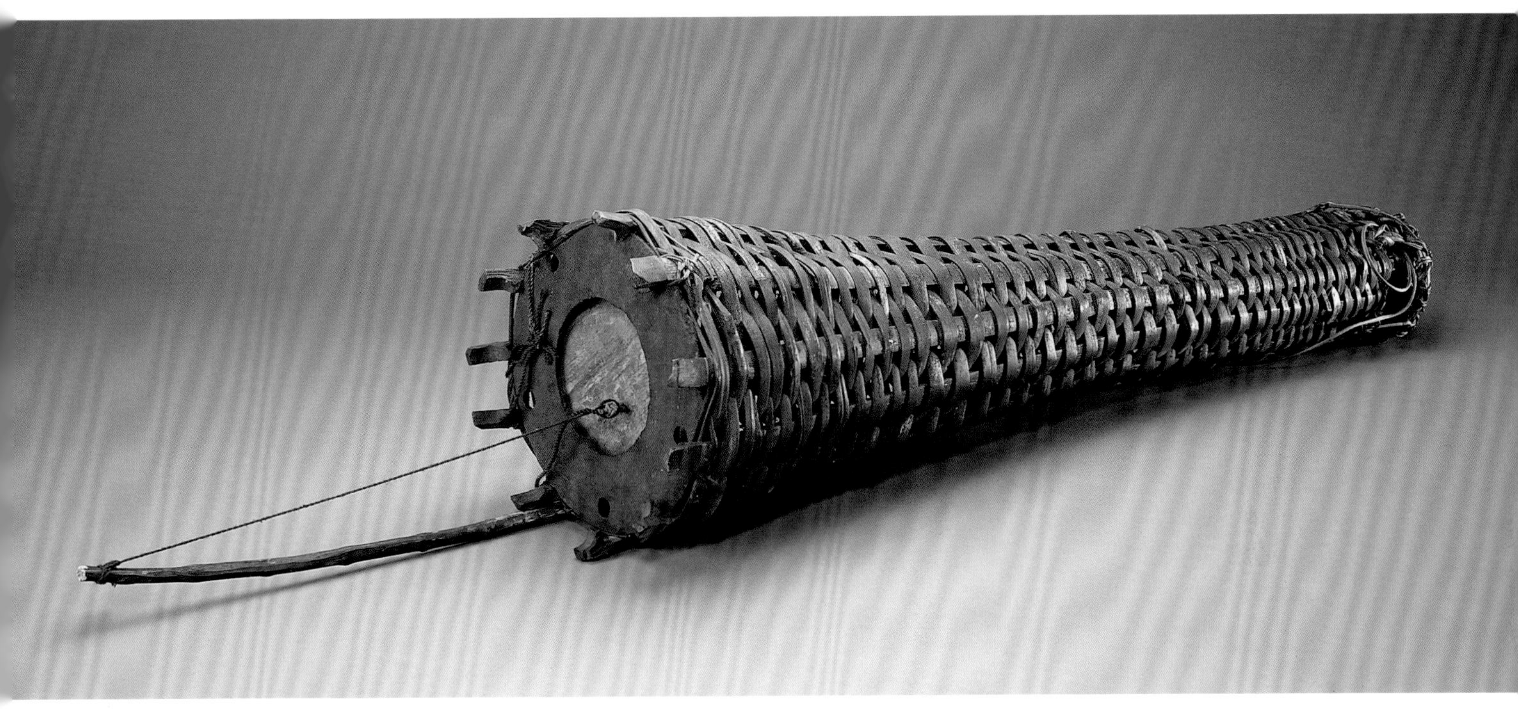

Catalog Number 40

Trap for eels, *udal*
Ifugao
Plaited construction
Bamboo, vine
Length 130 cm
FMCH X78.2350; Gift of Helen and Dr. Robert Kuhn

Used for catching eels in large streams, this trap has a spring-loaded cover at its mouth. The eel, attracted by bait consisting of small fish or worms, passes through the mouth of the trap, triggers the spring, and is trapped as the cover closes.

Catalog Number 41

Man's rain cape, *innanga*
Ifugao
Plaited construction with added twining
Rattan, *abnut* fiber from the *bangi* palm
Length 89 cm
FMCH X78.2421; Gift of Helen and Dr. Robert Kuhn

Men working in the rice terraces use a fiber cape to protect themselves from the cold, drenching rains that frequently fall in the highlands. The Ifugao usually fashion their capes out of *abnut*, the hairy fiber taken from the leafstalk margins of the *bangi* palm. The Bontoc and Kalinga make similar capes using cogon, a coarse grass that covers large areas of the highlands, or shreds of beaten bark fiber.

Cat. no. 41, back

FIGURE 4.20
A Kalinga woman wears a rain cape made of cogon grass while working in a flooded rice field. 1978.

Catalog Number 42

Woman's basket and rain cape,
tudung
Ifugao
Sewn construction
Pandanus leaf, rattan
Height 78 cm
FMCH X78.2336; Gift of Helen and
Dr. Robert Kuhn

Women in many parts of the Cordillera use a trough-shaped basket that doubles as a rain cape when it is inverted over the head. The basket is constructed of a layer of pandanus leaves (*ga-ad* in Ifugao) sandwiched between inner and outer frameworks of rattan. This type of basket is particularly useful for transporting wet rice seedlings at transplanting time. When the woman carries the basket on her head, its thick waterproof layers prevent the muck that adheres to the roots from dripping down over her. These baskets are also made in smaller sizes for carrying a variety of produce.

Cat. no. 42, back

FIGURE 4.21
An Ibaloi woman models the way in which the burden basket can be used as a rain cape. Early twentieth century. Day Collection, Fowler Museum of Cultural History.

Catalog Number 43

Man's sun or rain hat, *hallidung*
Ifugao
Plaited construction
Bamboo, rattan, resin
Diameter 47 cm
FMCH X78.2218; Gift of Helen and Dr. Robert Kuhn

Large round plaited hats, including the Ifugao *hallidung* and the Bontoc *sagfi*, are made by various Cordillera groups. The *hallidung* and *sagfi* are probably modeled after similar hats made by lowland Ilocanos. The *hallidung* functions primarily as a sun hat, but it is also covered with a layer of resin to make it waterproof. The Ifugao make a sealer for hats and other waterproof baskets by combining mud with sap collected from the *bulon* tree.

Cat. no. 43, underside of hat

Catalog Number 44

Hat, *soklong*
Bontoc
Coiled construction
Rattan, hair
Width 21 cm
FMCH X86.3371; Gift of Helen and Dr. Robert Kuhn

Like the Ifugao *ulbung*, or rice basket (cat. nos. 4, 5), the Bontoc married man's hat (*soklong*) is one of the few types of baskets made in the Cordillera using the coiling technique. According to Jenks, the form of the hat varied from village to village:

> The suk-lang is made in nearly all pueblos in the Bontoc culture area. It does not extend uninterruptedly to the western border, however, since it is not worn at all in Agawa, and in some other pueblos near the Lepanto border, as Fidelisan and Genugan, it has a rival in the headband.... The suk-lang varies in shape from the fez-like ti-no-od of Bontoc and Samoki, through various hemisperical forms, to the low flat hats developing eastward and perfected in the last mountains west of the Rio Grande de Cagayan. [1905, 111]

This elaborate style of *soklong* with a tuft of horse or human hair on top is made and worn in the Sagada region.

Cat. no. 44

Catalog Number 45

Nightcap, *kutla-u*
Bontoc
Plaited construction
Bamboo, rattan
Length 18 cm
FMCH X78.2472; Gift of Helen and Dr. Robert Kuhn

The *kutla-u* is a Bontoc nightcap, traditionally worn by both men and women. The long locks once favored by both sexes were wound inside the hat. The hat has been recorded as both a cushioning device for the head and a means to prevent infestation by lice, although Jenks wrote that he "was unable to get any reason from the Igorot for their use, save that they were worn by their ancestors" (1905, 113).

Catalog Number 46

Hat for bachelor, *soklong*
Bontoc
Twined construction
Rattan, boars' teeth, dogs' teeth
Width 14 cm
FMCH X96.5.53; Bequest of
Alan Rose

This colorful style of hat, decorated with boars' tusks and dogs' teeth, is a mark of the Bontoc bachelor. Similar hats are sometimes decorated with chicken feathers as well. The donning of his first *soklong* was a rite of passage for a Bontoc boy: "Up to age six or seven years the Igorot boys are as naked as when born. At that time they put on the suk-lang, the basket-work hat worn at the back of the head, held in place by a cord attached at both sides and passing across the forehead and usually hidden by the front hair" (Jenks 1905, 111). Bontoc men's hats double as "pockets" for personal items such as smoking supplies, which are tucked under the hat.

Cat. no. 46, detail

Catalog Number 47

Hat, *kattagang*
Kalinga
Plaited construction
Width 14 cm
FMCH X96.1.71; Gift of the Ventura County Museum of History and Art

The small, flat Kalinga man's hat is colorful, decorated with geometric patterns worked in red, yellow, and black. At least one author has linked its designs to Moorish forms of ornamentation (Linker 1961, 33).

Catalog Number 48

Amulet, *kiwil* or *agayok*
Ifugao
Plaited construction
Rattan
Height 7 cm
FMCH X91.5653;
Mr. and Mrs. Louis Marienthal

People of the Cordillera carry various types of magical charms. Among the Ifugao, a charm known as *kiwil* is believed to make its owner invulnerable to weapons. An *agayok* is a love charm that causes women to be sexually attracted to a man. Both of these charms usually consist of an object such as a special stone, a tektite found in the landscape, or a bezoar from the body of a slaughtered animal. Some Ifugao claim that the location of a charm is revealed to them in dreams. Another type of love charm (*amamulilit*) is made from the body of a species of small lizard that, according to traditional lore, gathers women's hair at the bathing place.

Whatever the material of the charm itself, it is frequently wrapped with rattan braiding, as in the case of this amulet. It is then carried in the owner's bag or in a knot in his loincloth. Very small charms are sometimes even inserted under the skin of the owner's arm. Without knowing what is inside the rattan covering and what it meant to its owner, it is impossible to know whether this charm was a *kiwil* or an *agayok*. Both are quite rare in museum collections, as the owners are normally unwilling to part with them or even to acknowledge their existence.

Catalog Number 49

Pouch for betel-chewing supplies,
upig
Ifugao
Plaited construction
Rattan
Length 20 cm
x78.2212a,b; Gift of Helen and
Dr. Robert Kuhn

The *upig* is a small flat pouch of finely plaited rattan, used by women to carry personal items such as betel-chewing supplies. It is tucked into a fold in the top of the woman's wraparound skirt.

Catalog Number 50

Basket for tobacco and personal supplies, *kupit*
Bontoc
Plaited construction
Rattan, bamboo, resin
Length 24 cm.
FMCH x78.2324a–c; Gift of Helen and Dr. Robert Kuhn

The *kupit* is one of the most intricately structured baskets made in the Cordillera. It normally consists of three or more shaped pieces that fit snugly together to form separate compartments. The compartment at the bottom of the container, which is the largest, can be used for carrying rice and other food to the fields for lunch. The middle compartment is for tobacco supplies and perhaps matches or other handy items used during the course of the day. There may be an additional "secret" compartment for storing valuables. The saddle-shaped top of the basket allows it to be cradled easily under the arm, and a coating of resin makes it waterproof.

Cat. no. 50

FIGURE 4.22
The man at the center of this Bontoc group, which posed for a photograph circa 1890, wears a *kupit* under his arm. Reproduced from Meyer and Schadenberg (1891, pl. 35).

Notes to the Text

Chapter 1

I wish to thank Harold Conklin for reading and commenting on an earlier version of this manuscript and for generously sharing his time and expertise. I am also grateful to Roy Hamilton for substantive comments and suggestions that skillfully steered this essay into its final form.

1. Scott's argument is partly based on the earlier writings of the Filipino scholar Dr. Trinidad Pardo de Tavera (see Jenks 1905, 27), who submits that "Igorot" derives from the root word *golot*, meaning "mountain chain," and the prefix *i*, meaning "dweller in" or "people of," hence "mountaineer."

2. Barton (1922, 418) describes this class structure and gives names for the upper (*kadangyan*), the middle (*natumok*), and lower (*nawatwat*) classes; but these terms are in dispute among current authorities, and *natumok*, in particular, is not recognized today.

3. The essential ingredients of a betel chew are the leaf of the betel pepper plant (*Piper betle*), the nut of the areca palm (*Areca catechu*), and lime (calcium hydroxide). Chewing tobacco or other flavoring ingredients are sometimes added.

4. Residual effects of the Saint Louis Exposition of 1904 on Americans who had visited the fair as young children and on contemporary Filipino-American descendants of Igorots who had been exhibited at the fair are explored in recently completed documentary films by Eric Breitbart and Mary Lance (1994) and Marlon Fuentes (1995).

5. Technically, "rice beer" is the proper term, as the beverage is produced through fermentation of grain, but "rice wine" has been in common use since the earliest descriptions in English by travelers and ethnologists.

6. Many contemporary Igorots have become Christian, and many fulfill important social, political, and educational roles in modern Philippine society.

Chapter 2

Conversations with Anthony Baguiwet of Tanulong and Edwardo Biag of Sagada have been helpful in providing perspective and information, and their help is hereby gratefully acknowledged. Conversations with Julio Tindungan of Ifugao, Miguel Suguiyao of Kalinga and Charles Enciso of Apayao during the second Igorot International Consultation in Washington, D.C., in July 1997 have also been helpful in providing a feel for the similarities and differences, and the functions, of baskets in the northern Luzon highlands as a whole. I thank them for their generosity during such a busy and hectic time. The accompanying photographs were taken by my wife, Carolyn, whose generosity and assistance are likewise greatly appreciated.

1. Most of the northern Luzon mountain country was encompassed in the original Mountain Province that existed from 1908 to 1966, a political unit set up by the American colonial authorities for the administration and governance of the indigenous population, generically referred to as Igorots. "Igorot" means people of or from the mountains. Today the area composed of the original Mountain Province plus Abra Province is popularly called the Cordillera Administrative Region (CAR).

2. Since the 1960s, plastic and metal (aluminum and tin) containers and fabric bags and knapsacks have become easily available and have replaced indigenous baskets to a considerable degree. The era of pervasiveness for the basket among the Fidelisan and Tanulong peoples may therefore be said to have ended during the 1950s.

3. These designations began during the Spanish period in the Philippines (1565–1898) and continued through the American and contemporary periods.

4. Missionaries from the Episcopal Church of the United States seated at Sagada, some 6 or 7 kilometers from Fidelisan and Tanulong, worked in the area intensively beginning in 1904. This resulted in a significant measure of Christianization and acculturation. Bangaan, Kodokod, Palidan, and Aguid are Fidelisan settlements that grew directly and indirectly from this missionary effort. Madongo and Nadatngan are the analogous ones for Tanulong.

5. The Fidelisan settlements are: Pedlisan or Fidelisan (the original or mother village), Pide, Aguid, Kodokod, Palidan, and Bangaan, while the Tanulong villages are Tanowong or Tanulong (the mother village), Cadatayan, Madongo, and Nadatngan.

6. Among the major characteristics of this type of social organization are bilateral descent or reckoning of relatives and independent nuclear families. See George Peter Murdock's groundbreaking book, *Social Structure*, for the definitive definition of the Eskimo type of social organization.

7. The notion of the sacred and the profane is propounded in Emile Durkheim's highly influential book, *The Elementary Forms of the Religious Life* (1961).

Chapter 3

1. The fieldwork for this paper was conducted in Banaue, Ifugao Province, from December 1994 to September 1995. The author acknowledges the financial support for this research provided by the Social Sciences and Humanities Research Council of Canada, doctoral fellowship, and by the Canada-ASEAN Centre, Academic Support Program.

2. *Bacnang* is an imported Ilocano term that identifies the upper class who have acquired their wealth through their own economic initiatives, such as craft making, rather than through inheritance.

3. Artisans buying rough rattan from market vendors purchase it in large bundles that have been subdivided into fourteen smaller sections. Those proficient in cleaning the rattan can prepare one small section in one to two hours. The women making small decorated animal containers and trays, for example, require one-half to one section of rattan. The cleaning thus adds one to two hours to each piece in preparation time.

4. In some instances, artisans may also get cash advances from those traders with whom they regularly conduct business. As many artisans earn just enough to cover their subsistence needs, some may find themselves in a cycle of debt to the trader when the value of their cash advances is greater than the value of the products they deliver.

5. The original color of bamboo and rattan ranges from beige to light or sandy brown. Over time and with use, the natural oils from food, from handling the basket, and from exposure to smoke from cooking fires turns these materials a golden to dark brown-black color. This patina speaks of the age of the piece and is in demand by tourists. Some basket makers sell their used baskets to traders in town or use them as a

"trade-in" on their purchase of new baskets, which they often prefer. The used baskets are then sold to tourists as "antiques," although they may only have been used for six to eight months. Indeed, in their effort to boost tourist sales, many shop owners artificially age their baskets by applying a tinted coal tar finish to new baskets and smoking them over a fire until the desired color is achieved.

6. *Baki* is the general Ifugao term for a local ritual. Each ritual, however, is individually named depending upon its purpose and the number of pigs butchered.

7. My analysis of the life history of objects such as baskets has been inspired by Igor Kopytoff's examples of the biographies of a Renoir painting and of a grass hut in Zaire (1986, 67). Inspiration has also come from the approach of the curators of *The Levy Legacy*, an exhibition mounted in early 1997 at the McMaster Museum of Art, Hamilton, Ontario, Canada. The documentation for each artwork outlined the object's own personal life history (e.g., place of purchase, comments of artist and past owners, where published).

8. Lynn Stephen (1996, 393) has similarly noted that the contemporary production of Zapotec weavings in Teotitlán del Valle, Mexico, provides artisans with opportunities not only to increase their incomes but also to nurture and maintain their social and cultural institutions.

References Cited

Bacdayan, Albert S.

1970 "Religious Conversion and Social Change: A Northern Luzon Case." *Practical Anthropology* 17: 119–27.

1974 "Securing Water for Drying Rice Terraces: Irrigation, Community Organization, and Expanding Social Relationships in a Western Bontoc Group, Philippines." *Ethnology* 13: 247–60. Also published as "Mountain Irrigators in the Philippines," in *Irrigation and Agricultural Development in Asia*, edited by E. Walter Coward, Jr., 172–85. Ithaca: Cornell University Press, 1980.

1977 "Mechanistic Cooperation and Sexual Equality among the Western Bontoc." In *Sexual Stratification: A Cross-Cultural View*, edited by Alice Schlegel, 270–91. New York: Columbia University Press.

1995 "A Preference for Rice." *Discovery* 25 (2): 20–25.

Barton, Roy Franklin

1919 "Ifugao Economics." *University of California Publications in American Archaeology and Ethnology* 15 (1): 385–446.

1922 *Ifugao Economics*. Berkeley: University of California Press.

1930 *The Half-Way Sun: Life Among the Headhunters of the Philippines*. New York: Brewer and Warren.

1946 *The Religion of the Ifugaos*. Memoir Series, vol. 65. Menasha, Wisconsin: American Anthropological Association.

1949 *The Kalingas*. Chicago: The University of Chicago Press.

1955 *The Mythology of the Ifugaos*. Memoirs, vol. 46. Philadelphia: American Folklore Society.

Breitbart, Eric, and Mary Lance

1994 *A World on Display*. New Deal Films, released 1996, videocassette.

Capistrano-Baker, Florina H.

1994 *Art of Island Southeast Asia: The Fred and Rita Richman Collection in the Metropolitan Museum of Art*. New York: The Metropolitan Museum of Art.

1995 "Divine Spheres of Protection: Shields of the Philippines." In *Protection, Power, and Display: Shields of Island Southeast Asia and Melanesia*, edited by A. Tavarelli. Boston: Boston College Museum of Art.

Clifford, James

1988 *The Predicament of Culture: Twentieth-Century Ethnography, Literature, and Art.* Cambridge, Mass.: Harvard University Press.

Cole, Fay-Cooper

1922 *The Tinguian: Social, Religious, and Economic Life.* Anthropological Series, vol. 8, no. 2, publication 209. Chicago: Field Museum of Natural History.

Cole, Fay-Cooper, and Berthold Laufer

1912 *Chinese Pottery in the Philippines.* Anthropological Series, vol. 8, no. 1, publication 162. Chicago: Field Museum of Natural History.

Conklin, Harold C.

1980 *Ethnographic Atlas of Ifugao: A Study of Environment, Culture, and Society in North Luzon.* New Haven: Yale University Press.

Dominguez, Virginia R.

1986 "The Marketing of Heritage," Review Article. *American Ethnologist* 13 (3): 546–55.

Durkheim, Emile

1961 *The Elementary Forms of the Religious Life.* Translated by Joseph Ward Swain. New York: Collier Books.

Ellis, George R.

1981 "Arts and Peoples of the Northern Philippines." In *The People and Art of the Philippines*, edited by Father Gabriel Casal and Regaldo T. Jose, Jr. Los Angeles: UCLA Museum of Cultural History.

Franklin, Ursula

1992 *The Real World of Technology.* Toronto: Anansi.

Fuentes, Marlon

1995 *Bontoc Eulogy.* New York, The Cinema Guild, videocassette.

Gordon, Beverly

1986 "The Souvenir: Messenger of the Extraordinary." *Journal of Popular Culture* 20: 135–46.

Jenista, Frank Lawrence

1987 *The White Apos: American Governors on the Cordillera Central.* Quezon City: New Day.

Jenks, Albert E.

1905 *The Bontoc Igorot.* Manila: Bureau of Public Printing.

Jules-Rosette, Bennetta

1986 "Aesthetics and Market Demand: The Structure of the Tourist Art Market in Three African Settings." *African Studies Review* 29 (1): 41–59.

Karnow, Stanley

1989 *In Our Image: America's Empire in the Philippines.* New York: Ballantine Books.

Keesing, F. M., and M. Keesing

1934 *Taming Philippine Headhunters: A Study of Government and Cultural Change in Northern Luzon.* Stanford: Stanford University Press.

Kipling, Rudyard

1899 "The White Man's Burden." *McClure's Magazine* 12 (Feb.) <http://www.rochester.ican.net/~fjzwick/kipling/kipling.html>. In Jim Zwick, ed., *Anti-Imperialism in the United States, 1898–1935* <http://www.rochester.ican.net/~fjzwick/ail98-35.html> (January 1996).

Kopytoff, Igor

1986 "The Cultural Biography of Things: Commoditization as Process." In *The Social Life of Things: Commodities in Cultural Perspective*, edited by Arjun Appadurai, 64–94. Cambridge: Cambridge University Press.

Lane, Robert F.

1986 *Philippine Basketry: An Appreciation*. Manila: Bookmark.

Linker, Ruth

1961 "Philippine Hats." *Expedition*: 30–36.

Meyer, A. B., and A. Schadenberg

1891 *Album von Philippinen-Typen: Nord Luzon*. Dresden: Stengel & Markert.

Moss, C. R.

1920 *Nabaloi Law and Ritual*. Berkeley: University of California Press.

Murdock, George P.

1960 *Social Structure*. New York: Macmillan.

Newell, Leonard E.

1993 *Batad Ifugao Dictionary*. Manila: Linguistic Society of the Philippines.

Ortner, Sherry B.

1973 "On Key Symbols." *American Anthropologist* 75 (5): 1338–46.

1978 *Sherpas through Their Rituals*. Cambridge: Cambridge University Press.

Reid, Lawrence A.

1976 *Bontok-English Dictionary*. Canberra: Department of Linguistics, Research School of Pacific Studies, The Australian National University.

Russell, Susan D., and Clark E. Cunningham

1989 "Introduction: Social Change, Cultural Identity, and Ritual Response." In *Changing Lives, Changing Rites: Ritual and Social Dynamics in Philippine and Indonesian Uplands*, edited by Susan D. Russell and Clark E. Cunningham, 1–16. Ann Arbor: University of Michigan.

Schadenberg, Alexander

1889 "Beiträge zur Kenntniss der im Innern Nordluzons lebenden Stämme." *Zeitschrift für Ethnologie* 21: 674–700.

Scott, William Henry

1966 *On the Cordillera: A Look at the Peoples and Cultures of the Mountain Province*. Manila: MCS Enterprises.

1974 *The Discovery of the Igorots: Spanish Contacts with the Pagans of Northern Luzon*. Foreword by H. C. Conklin. Quezon City: New Day; rev. ed. 1977.

Stephen, Lynn

1996 Reprint. "Export Markets and Their Effects on Indigenous Craft Production: The Case of the Weavers of Teotitlán del Valle, Mexico." In *Textile Traditions of Mesoamerica and the Andes: An Anthology*, edited by Margot Blum Schevill, Janet Catherine Berlo, and Edward B. Dwyer, 381–402. Austin: University of Texas Press. Original edition, New York: Garland, 1991.

Worcester, Dean C.

1912 "Head-Hunters of Northern Luzon." *The National Geographic Magazine* 23 (9): 833–930.

Illustration Credits

FIGURE 1.1	Roy W. Hamilton	FIGURE 4.4	Don Cole, © Fowler Museum of Cultural History
FIGURE 1.2	Roy W. Hamilton		
FIGURE 1.3	Charles LeNoir	FIGURE 4.5	Roy W. Hamilton
FIGURE 1.4	© David L. Fuller	FIGURE 4.6	Roy W. Hamilton
FIGURE 1.5	© Harold C. Conklin*	FIGURE 4.7	Roy W. Hamilton
FIGURE 1.6	© Harold C. Conklin*	FIGURE 4.9	© Harold C. Conklin
FIGURE 1.7	Roy W. Hamilton	FIGURE 4.11	H. Otley Beyer
FIGURE 1.9	Charles LeNoir	FIGURE 4.12	© Harold C. Conklin
FIGURE 1.10	Roy W. Hamilton	FIGURE 4.15	© Harold C. Conklin*
FIGURE 1.11	Charles LeNoir	FIGURE 4.16	Charles LeNoir
FIGURE 1.12	© Harold C. Conklin*	FIGURE 4.18	Roy W. Hamilton
FIGURE 1.17	Roy W. Hamilton	FIGURE 4.19	Roy W. Hamilton
FIGURES 2.1–2.19	Carolyn Bacdayan	FIGURE 4.20	Charles LeNoir
FIGURES 3.1–3.21	B. Lynne Milgram	CATALOG NOS. 1–50	Don Cole, © Fowler Museum of Cultural History
FIGURE 4.2	Roy W. Hamilton		

* These photographs were originally published in Conklin (1980, figs. 50, 80, 49, 67).

Contributors

Florina H. Capistrano-Baker received her doctorate from the Department of Art History and Archaeology at Columbia University in 1997. From 1988 to 1994 she was a member of the curatorial staff at the Metropolitan Museum of Art, and she subsequently taught the history of non-Western art at Northwestern University. She recently assumed the directorship of the Museo ng Maynila (Manila Museum), Philippines. Capistrano-Baker's current research focuses on issues of identity and the colonial experience.

Albert S. Bacdayan was born and raised in Bangaan, a Fidelisan village. He received his early education in the Philippines and graduated from the University of the Philippines in Quezon City. After obtaining a doctoral degree in anthropology from Cornell University in 1967, he began teaching at the University of Kentucky, where he ultimately served as director of graduate studies and chairman of the Department of Anthropology. Following his retirement in 1989, he moved to Lyme, Connecticut, where he pursues his interest in small-scale organic agriculture.

B. Lynne Milgram holds a doctorate in anthropology from York University, Toronto. Since 1980 she has been the associate curator for Asian textiles at the Museum for Textiles, Toronto; currently she holds a two-year postdoctoral fellowship in the Department of Anthropology at the University of Toronto. She is the editor, with P. Van Esterik, of *The Transformative Power of Cloth in Southeast Asia* (1994) and the author of the exhibition catalog *Narratives in Cloth: Embroidered Textiles from Aomori, Japan* (1993).

Roy W. Hamilton is the curator of Southeast Asian and Oceanic Collections at the UCLA Fowler Museum of Cultural History. He is the editor and principal author of *Gift of the Cotton Maiden: Textiles of Flores and the Solor Islands* (1994) and *From the Rainbow's Varied Hue: Textiles of the Southern Philippines* (1998). He is currently working on projects focusing on the paraphernalia associated with betel chewing and on rice agriculture in a number of Asian countries.